Romano Guardini

Proclaiming the Sacred
in a Modern World

January 1996

To Michael Sullivan,

my CSC "dean" since 1964

who serves the church as priest,

teacher, historian, and brother

with best wishes, Bob

Edited by
Robert A. Krieg, CSC

D1287888

Liturgy Training Publications

Acknowledgments

Chapter four is a revised version of an essay that originally appeared in Wilhelm Geerlings and Max Scheler (eds.), *Kirche sein* (Freiburg im Breisgau: Herder, 1994), 93–100. It is printed here with the permission of Herder Verlag.

All quotations from scripture are taken from the New Revised Standard Version of the Bible (New York: Oxford University Press, 1989).

Acquisitions editor: Victoria M. Tufano
Production editor: Deborah Bogaert
Design: Judy Sweetwood, Barb Rohm
Production Artist: Mark Hollopeter
This book was typeset in Garamond and printed by Versa Press, Inc.

Printed in the United States of America.

Library of Congress Cataloging-in-Publications Data

Romano Guardini: proclaiming the sacred in a modern world/edited by Robert A. Kreig.
　　p. cm.
　　Includes bibliographical references.
　　1. Guardini, Romano, 1885–1968—Congresses. 2. Catholic Church—Doctrines—History—20th century—Congresses. 3. Catholic Church—Liturgy—Congresses. I. Krieg, Robert Anthony, 1946–
BX4705.G6265R66　　1995
230'.2'092—dc20
[B]
ISBN 1-56854-106-6　　　　　　　　　　　　　　　　　　　　95-25155
GUARD　　　　　　　　　　　　　　　　　　　　　　　　　　　　CIP

Contents

At least once or twice a year, thousands of people stream into South Bend's convention hall, the Century Center, to attend exhibits and trade shows for antiquarian plates, antique furniture, old baseball cards, canceled postage stamps, rare coins and just about anything else that is aged and unusual. For these convention-goers, some of whom travel hundreds of miles for these jamborees, the basic principle seems to be "the older, odder and more out of date, the better."

On October 7 and 8, 1994, approximately 50 people gathered at the University of Notre Dame's Center for Continuing Education to participate in a conference on the life and work of Romano Guardini (1885 – 1968). As we assembled, some of us wondered whether we were involved in a ritual not unlike the in-gatherings at the Century Center, just a couple miles away. Were we basically treating Guardini as though he were an antique doll? Were we acting on an unconscious longing to return to 1950s Catholicism, and were we implicitly attracted to Guardini's writings according to the ideal of "the older, the odder and more out of date, the better"?

From the outset, the planners of this conference were clear about two goals. First, we wanted to celebrate the twenty-fifth anniversary of Guardini's death. In fact, we gathered for the twenty-sixth anniversary because, as we learned, planning for even a small conference takes time.

Second, we wanted to fill a void. To our knowledge, a formal conference on Romano Guardini's life and writings had never been held in Canada or the United States. Throughout the 1950s and 1960s, tens of thousands of Catholics in North America had read English translations of books and articles by Guardini, and they eventually felt a debt of gratitude to this theologian for preparing them, at least to some extent, for the changes in the church brought about by the Second Vatican Council. But North American Catholics had never publicly expressed their gratitude to Guardini by means of a formal conference. They had lost track of Guardini during his last years, for by then they were focused on post-conciliar theology and the rapid changes in the liturgy and parish life, as well as on the social and political turmoil of the late 1960s. In light of this neglect, we agreed that something had to occur to mark the twenty-fifth (okay, the twenty-sixth) anniversary of Guardini's death.

Nevertheless, until the opening of our conference, the thought passed among us that we were really coming together for old-times' sake. Perhaps our true, though unwitting, aim was to swap memories of reading Guardini's books as though our recollections were dog-eared baseball cards or Civil War coins.

Much to our delight, from the first moment of our conference until the last, we discovered something wonderful. Those who had assembled in the conference hall had not come for the sake of nostalgia nor in reaction to the current state of affairs in the church. All of us had come to the conference to give thanks to God for Romano Guardini and to see how this scholar's wisdom could be remembered and then directed like a beam of light toward the present and future. Our common question was not only What did Guardini say about the liturgy or the church? but also, What can we still learn from Guardini's writings that will help us pursue, in our circumstances, Guardini's vision of church and liturgy?

The answers that we heard in our formal presentations and also in our informal conversations were heartening and enlightening to all of us. For this reason, we are now making the conference's papers available to the many people who, like ourselves, still feel a debt of gratitude for Guardini's work and also would like to benefit even now from his learning.

The chapters in this book are meant to shed light on Guardini's world, life, thought and influence. In chapter one, "Fires in the Night: Germany 1920–1950," Heinz R. Kuehn recalls what life was like for Guardini and for Kuehn himself in Berlin during the Weimar Republic and the Third Reich. Chapter two, Robert A. Krieg's "A Precursor's Life and Work," provides a biographical sketch of Guardini from his birth in Verona to his death in Munich. In chapter three, "The Major Theological Themes of Romano Guardini," Arno Schilson highlights Guardini's thought on the interrelationship of faith and culture, the nature of the church and the mystery of Jesus Christ.

Chapter four, "North American Catholics' Reception of Romano Guardini's Writings," also by Robert A. Krieg, reviews the sequence in which Guardini's texts appeared in English and their impact on their readers, especially Thomas Merton. In chapter five, "Romano Guardini as Sapiential Theologian," Lawrence S. Cunningham explains Guardini's bold vision of theology as an imaginative synthesis of the riches of the Catholic spiritual tradition, critical systematic study and the analysis of great works of literature. In chapter six, "Romano Guardini's View of Liturgy: A Lens for Our Time," Kathleen Hughes illuminates Guardini's insights into the character of worship and discusses how these truths apply to worship today.

Chapter seven, "Encounters with Romano Guardini," fills in our understanding of Guardini's life and thought by providing the remembrances of four people who had direct contact with Guardini. In "Romano Guardini in Berlin," Regina Kuehn remembers her interactions with and impressions of Romano Guardini when she studied with him and served as his assistant at the University of Berlin. In "Romano Guardini in Munich," Albert K. Wimmer reflects on what he learned at the University of Munich as he listened to Guardini's lectures. In "The 'Sacred Signs' of Romano Guardini," Gertrud Mueller Nelson recalls meeting Guardini in Munich after having been nurtured on his ideas by her parents, who had been closely associated with the theologian in Germany. Finally, in "Romano Guardini's *Akademische Feier* in 1964," Thomas F. O'Meara recounts how, at the retirement ceremony for Guardini at the University of Munich, the aged theologian stepped aside and gave his academic chair to his successor, Karl Rahner (1904 – 1984).

In keeping with Guardini's ability to unite inspiration with exposition, this book concludes in chapter eight with a meditation by Gertrud Mueller Nelson on "Romano Guardini's Spirit Today." Then, a bibliography provides a selection of Guardini's books in English and also a selection of articles in English on Guardini. The book ends with biographical sketches of its contributors.

We wish to acknowledge in gratitude that our conference on Romano Guardini and hence the papers that constitute this book were made possible by a major grant from the Paul M. and Barbara Henkels Visiting Scholar Series of the College of Arts and Letters at the University of Notre Dame and by supporting grants from the University's Provost, Timothy O'Meara; the chairman of the Theology Department, Lawrence S. Cunningham; the director of the Marten Program for Homiletics and Liturgics, John A. Melloh; and the William K. Warren professor of theology, Thomas F. O'Meara.

Also, we want to thank Gabe Huck, director of Liturgy Training Publications (LTP), for enthusiastically sponsoring this publication. Moreover, we are grateful to Victoria Tufano, senior acquisitions editor of LTP, for proposing that the conference's papers appear in print and then preparing the manuscript for publication. For a long time, LTP has taken many significant steps to implement a vision of church and liturgy in North America that bears a family resemblance to Guardini's vision. This similarity is immediately evident when one scans LTP's catalog of publications. We are delighted, too, that LTP is collaborating with Heinz R. Kuehn on an anthology of Guardini's most significant writings, to be published in early 1997.

One last comment. At the Guardini Conference, some of us were painfully aware of the absence of Mark Searle (1941 – 1992). For over a decade, Mark worked tirelessly among us to communicate by means of lectures, workshops, articles and books his rich insights into worship, the sacraments and the Christian life — insights that sprang in part from the writings of Romano Guardini. As a result, Mark helped start and direct today's "new liturgical movement" in North America (see Lawrence J. Madden, "A New Liturgical Movement," in *America* 170 [September 10, 1994], 16 – 19). While missing Mark, we are consoled by our belief that Mark has now joined Romano Guardini in the communion of saints in giving eternal glory and praise to God.

It is our hope that all who read these pages will find themselves walking not into a crowd of antiquarians but into a conversation among lovers of Christian wisdom who have turned to the life and writings of Romano Guardini in order to receive strength and light to explore the opportunities of today and tomorrow.

Robert A. Krieg, CSC

Chapter One

Fires in the Night: Germany 1920–1950

Heinz R. Kuehn

I n this first chapter I will sketch some of the contours of the political, religious and social landscape of Germany between the 1920s and 1950s, with a focus on Berlin. This is the city and the time in which I grew up and came to maturity, and which formed the background for Guardini's most productive years. Since my remarks about a man who in many ways indelibly shaped my generation's vision of Catholicism and the post-modern world will be largely autobiographical and anecdotal, permit me a few words about my own background.

Although I am a native German, I am neither a native Berliner nor a "born Catholic." I was born in Bern, Switzerland, where my father had joined the German embassy after being wounded during the First World War and where he met and married my mother, who had been his secretary. She was Jewish but indifferent to religion; he came from a Protestant family but was an agnostic for much of his life. In 1920, my parents returned with me to Germany, where my sister was born a year later. After my parents were divorced in 1924, my mother settled with us in Berlin, where I lived until I emigrated to America in 1951. My sister and I went to schools where Protestant religious instruction was part of the curriculum. Our relationship to our father was close, and when he converted to Catholicism in the late 1920s, we eventually embraced the Catholic faith under his influence.

As the first foundation stone of my bridge to Guardini, let me add here that in 1923, the year before Berlin became my home for 27 years, Guardini had become Professor for Philosophy of Religion and Catholic Weltanschauung — or worldview — at the University of Berlin. Of course his name was meaningless to me, then a five-year-old boy, and, for that matter, to my parents. What matters here is that for the next 20 years he and I would see the same sights, hear the same sounds, read the same

1

newspapers, listen to the same radio programs and use the same city railways, buses and streetcars until, in 1943, he left the city for Mooshausen in rural southern Germany.

What did we see, hear and read? As the title of this chapter indicates, the memory of my childhood — indeed of the 32 years of my "German life" — is literally and symbolically a memory of fires in the night. The year 1919, the year I was born, saw the beginning of Germany's first experiment with a democratic form of government, under the name of the Weimar Republic. Its constitution created a firm foundation for democracy, but it was a foundation continuously under severe stress until it collapsed when Adolf Hitler came to power. Of the scores of political parties fighting for votes and a voice in government, three formed an uneasy governing coalition: one having a moderately liberal persuasion, one a moderately conservative one, and one, the Center Party, which represented political Catholicism, being a mixture of both.

The young Professor Guardini in 1926, three years after accepting the chair in the Philosophy of Religion and Catholic Weltanschauung at the University of Berlin.

The government faced an impossible task. Two million Germans had lost their lives during the war, and more than four million had been severely wounded. Germany was reeling under the crushing burden of the Treaty of Versailles, which had imposed on it hundreds of billions of dollars in war reparations, had split off one-eighth of its territory with a population of seven million and had given to France for 15 years its most productive industrial region, the Saarland. Equally disastrous, the governing coalition was under relentless attack from the radical left — the Communists and the radical Socialists — and from the radical right — the ultranationalists and the National Socialists, the Nazis. More importantly for our theme, the war had dealt a devastating blow to a Western world that still rested on an essentially Christian framework of values; the war had ushered in the era of nihilism, existentialism and relativism.

For the people, for us, the political reality of the Weimar Republic became tangible and audible in the streets, in the stores, in offices, schools and universities. The reality was of a fanatical, murderous, pitched battle for power, exemplified by the murders of Rosa Luxemburg and Karl Liebknecht, two leading figures in the radical Socialist movement, by army officers in 1919; of Matthias Erzberger, the most outstanding leader of the Center Party who had signed the armistice; and of Walter Rathenau, a brilliant Jew who had become foreign minister. In 1923, Hitler attempted a coup in Munich to force the Bavarian government to work against the Berlin government. The attempt failed, and Hitler was imprisoned in the fortress of Landsberg, where he wrote his infamous *Mein Kampf,* in which he spelled out his program for a Germany under Nazi dictatorship.

Much of this bloody turmoil was centered on Berlin, the capital. Many were the times when, on my way to school or to a store, I had to duck into a doorway or throw myself to the ground to seek protection from snipers or from a machine gun that began firing from a roof or window on a column of marchers whose banners bore the insignia of one or another party, mostly either the swastika or the hammer and sickle. In addition, there was inflation and rising unemployment, both of which reached with their consequences into every home except for those of the entrepreneurs and industrial barons. In 1923, for example, one former Goldmark was worth one trillion paper marks. And in 1930, unemployment rose to more than six million among a total population of some sixty million. Food riots broke out almost weekly. At home, my mother, my sister and I lived as much on barter as on her modest salary as a secretary, and still today, when it comes to paying for something in cash, I see before me the large cloth shopping bag stuffed with paper money I needed to buy one loaf of bread and a quarter pound of margarine.

Again, Guardini, too, lived and worked in Berlin during these years, even though he divided his time between that city and Burg Rothenfels. Did the events of those years influence his writings? There is no doubt that the bloody turmoil of these years left its mark on his work, particularly his studies of literature. In some of his books about literary figures, he speaks of Satan and his demons in an unequivocally biblical sense. His view of Western society between the end of World War I and the mid-1950s was that of a "wilderness." In his book *The End of the Modern World,* Guardini writes:

> In this wilderness all the abysses of the primeval times have opened up again.
> All the wild and choking growth of the forests again presses forward. All the
> monsters of the wilderness are roaming again, all the terrors of utter darkness.
> [Humanity] again faces chaos. This is all the more dreadful since most of us
> do not recognize it, because everywhere scientific experts are talking, machines
> are running perfectly and governments are functioning.[1]

However, there was also something else shaping his view of the world and religion during his years in Berlin and, according to his diaries and letters, not only filled many of his leisure hours but also found its way into his writings. Berlin during the Weimar Republic was the cultural center of Europe. Art, music, theater, the cinema and nightlife flourished. It was the time of the brilliant theater director Max Reinhardt, of the movie director Fritz Lang, of Marlene Dietrich and Greta Garbo, of the graphic artist and sculptor Käthe Kollwitz, of the conductors Wilhelm Furtwängler and Herbert von Karajan, of the Bauhaus School in architecture, of Berthold Brecht, Alfred Döblin, Ricarda Huch, and Heinrich and Thomas Mann.

Another element — a political element — of the Weimar Republic undoubtedly played a role in the course of Guardini's life by providing the atmosphere and giving him the elbow room he needed for the full development of his talents and the wide acceptance of what he had to offer. The Center Party, which on average received about 18 percent of the votes at election time, not only had considerable political power but also was a significant spiritual and intellectual force — not to mention its clout when it came to allocating the resources of the nation's budget. Consequently, the Catholic church flourished during the Weimar Republic. Money for new schools, convents and monasteries was readily available, there was an abundance of Catholic papers and magazines, and there was an organization for virtually every interest or cause that sought to make its voice heard in the marketplace. A man of Guardini's genius and vision had a ready-made audience enthusiastically receiving his books, which appeared in quick succession during this era — books such as *The Life of Faith, The Living God, The Church and the Catholic, Sacred Signs* and *The Spirit of the Liturgy,* to name only some of his most influential works.

Berlin during the Weimar Republic was the cultural center of Europe. Art, music, theater, the cinema and nightlife flourished.

With the crash of the New York Stock Exchange in October 1929 and the beginning of a worldwide depression, conditions in Germany went rapidly from bad to worse. Unemployment passed the six million mark, resulting in an explosive increase in membership in extremist parties on both the right and the left. In the 1928 elections, for example, the Nazis received 810,000 votes; two years later, in 1930, they received 6.5 million votes, about half the votes of the eligible voters. When the aging and near-senile president of the Weimar Republic, Paul von Hindenburg, reluctantly yielded to the pressures and intrigues of his son and members of his inner circle and appointed Adolf Hitler to the office of Reich Chancellor on January 30, 1933, Germany's first experiment with democracy came to an end and the Nazi dictatorship began.

On the evening of that day, I, then 13 years old, stood among the crowd that had gathered in front of Berlin's Chancery building. When Hitler appeared briefly on the balcony and waved to the screaming and cheering throng, I saw for the first time the man whose deeds have left an indelible mark on the history of the modern world. I saw him again face to face a couple of months later when I had become a student at a boarding school in Potsdam. We participated in a ceremony at Potsdam's Garrison

Church at which Hitler and Hindenburg celebrated the so-called rebirth of a united Germany under Hitler's leadership. Two years after this episode, I was expelled from the boarding school because of my Jewish background, and that same year I converted to Catholicism. I was 14 years old.

With my conversion, Guardini became a presence whose impact on my thoughts and on the vision and practice of my faith grew steadily. I will give you five brief examples: my membership in the Catholic youth movement; my attendance of the Sunday Mass Guardini celebrated in Berlin's Students' Chapel; my membership in the Thomas Circle, one of the many Catholic groups that met clandestinely; my frequent visits to a small Benedictine convent on the southern outskirts of Berlin; and my attendance of the University of Tübingen.

Guardini had become an indispensable element in the struggle of the church not only to find a solid footing in the modern, secularized world, but, in the case of Nazi Germany, simply to survive intellectually, culturally and spiritually.

After my conversion, I immediately joined a Catholic organization of boys who attended the gymnasium, a classical school preparatory to the university. Founded by Jesuits and called *Neudeutschland,* or New Germany, this organization fostered patriotism, military discipline, asceticism and a vision of the world that combined Catholic universalism with German romanticism. Since one of the principal purposes of New Germany was to Christianize — or, if you will, Catholicize — what we were learning at the gymnasium according to Nazi ideology, particularly in the field of the humanities and the arts, our group meetings were chiefly devoted to reading and discussing classical German literature side by side with contemporary Catholic German authors. This was the time of the Renaissance of Catholic creative writing. My father, a historian and francophile, had already introduced me to writers such as Mauriac, Bernanos and Claudel, and now, at these meetings, I got to know also the works of Gertrud von LeFort, Reinhold Schneider and Werner Bergengruen. It was here — and now we have returned to our theme — that I became familiar with the writings of Guardini.

I have, of course, long forgotten which of his books we read and talked about. It could have been *The Life of Faith, Stendhal* or *Pascal for Our Time,* or possibly even *The Lord,* which appeared in 1937. The point I wish to make is this: Guardini's methods at Burg Rothenfels to achieve among young Catholics an understanding of the turbulent world in which they lived and an unequivocal commitment to the Catholic faith and the church were, of course, quite different from the ways in which New Germany approached this goal. The Jesuit leadership of New Germany, however, clearly recognized that Guardini had become an indispensable element in the struggle of the church not only to find a solid footing in the modern, secularized world, but, in the case of Nazi Germany, simply to survive intellectually, culturally and spiritually. We had no other Catholic author who made us see our world from the perspective of divine revelation as clearly, as cogently and as persuasively as did Guardini, teaching us at the same time to transform that understanding and vision into a daily, living reality.

I met Romano Guardini for the first time in person in the fall of 1938. By then I had graduated from the gymnasium, had obtained a furnished room in the Catholic Students' Home in return for some household chores and was waiting to be called up for the obligatory six-month stint in the Reich Labor Service. The Students' Chapel (St. Benedict) where Guardini celebrated Mass on Sundays and sometimes during the week, was located only a few blocks away from the Students' Home, and I became a regular attendee.

The chapel was a small, unadorned room located in the semi-basement of an apartment building. It had a few rows of chairs, a small, table-like, free-standing altar, and the only natural light came from a couple of oblong windows under its ceiling on the level of the street. Half a flight up from the chapel, on the first floor of the building, was a chapel reserved for Russian Orthodox services, and when, as sometimes happened, the Roman and Orthodox Masses were scheduled at the same time, the deep, sonorous voices of the Russian Orthodox choir formed something of a mystical, tonal background to our eucharistic celebration half a floor below.

If I wanted to explain in a few words what irresistibly drew me and the small congregation that came from all parts of Berlin to Guardini's Mass, it was simply this: He was a person who by his words and actions drew us into a world where the sacred became convincingly and literally tangible. His mere appearance radiated something for which I have no better word than *numinous;* in his presence one fell silent and became all attention. With him at the altar, the sacred table became the center of the universe. But was it a universe of fantasy? Of escape? Of religious sentiment that did not survive for 24 hours? Or was it the center of *our* universe, *our* daily reality?

Let me attempt an answer to that question with an experience that for me unforgettably connects the name and person of Guardini with my life under Nazi tyranny. On Monday, November 7, 1938, the third secretary of the German embassy in Paris was killed by a Polish Jew. The following Wednesday, as I was walking home from a meeting, I noticed in the sky a reddish glow that looked like the reflection of a huge fire. It was in the direction of the Kurfürstendamm, West Berlin's fashionable center of

Jewish stores, synagogues, theaters and residential quarters where my mother lived. I began to run, and as I turned the corner into the Kurfürstendamm, I smelled smoke and heard the crunching of broken glass under my feet. Flames shooting out of the roof of a synagogue in a side street lit up the stately avenue and revealed a ghastly sight. Wherever I looked, I saw the smashed display windows of stores and elegant boutiques, of restaurants and cafés, with brown-shirted storm troopers standing in front of them with wide-spread legs and folded arms. The sidewalks were covered with broken glass.

Small groups of passers-by and guests driven out of the restaurants and cafés looked at the devastation in stunned silence. Here and there a policeman stood motionless, with his eyes on the crowd. Trucks loaded with Storm Troopers raced up and down the avenue, and their screams of *"Juden raus!"* — "Out with the Jews!" — reverberated from the buildings. It was the famous, or infamous, *Kristallnacht,* the Night of the Broken Glass, during which 177 Jewish synagogues and 7,500 Jewish-owned stores were systematically burned down or otherwise destroyed in Germany and Austria.

When I arrived at my mother's apartment, I learned that she was safely spending the night in the home of some friends. The next morning I went to St. Benedict Chapel, where Guardini was scheduled to celebrate Mass. There I happened to meet my sister, and, as we were about to take our seats, someone said loudly as Guardini was approaching the altar, "Now let's get a foothold on reality again."

A foothold on reality? Nothing apparently was further from our daily and nightly reality than a liturgical action in a small room in the sub-basement of an apartment building. The Night of the Broken Glass was one reality; mass arrests, mass murders, and killings in clinics and hospitals of the old and the newborn considered by the Nazis unworthy of living was another; the fear for my mother's and her Jewish relatives' safety and their transportation to concentration camps was yet another reality.

As for the Catholic church, on Palm Sunday in 1937, Pius XI's encyclical *Mit brennender Sorge* (With Burning Sorrow) was read from the pulpits, attacking not only violations of the concordat but also the ideology and racial doctrines of the Third Reich. For Hitler, it amounted to a declaration of war. Priests' houses were searched, and many priests were deported to concentration camps. Catholic schools were closed, Catholic civil servants were dismissed, Catholic publications were liquidated or censored, and diocesan property was confiscated.

And yet for us, where we found the foothold that gave us the strength and courage to face, to endure and to resist a world in which the forces of evil, Satan and his demons, were reigning rampant, was in that small chapel, in the presence of a man whose words and actions made truth appear among us like a physical presence. The impact of the sacred action was all the more profound because Guardini celebrated the Mass *versus populum* — facing the people. It was a *Missa Recitata,* a Mass at which people responded aloud to the presider's prayers, something still new in those days, and we, the congregation, were the altar boys and girls answering his invitations to prayer. Guardini himself, in *The End of the Modern World,* which first appeared in 1950, formulated what he strongly felt but could not yet articulate:

> From an immediate religious viewpoint, liturgical cult produces an all-inclusive order of being. In every present moment of history, cult renews and makes real through symbolic forms the eternally valid fact of redemption.[2]

But in his *Berichte über mein Leben* (Reports about My Life), which appeared posthumously, Guardini specifically refers to the St. Benedict Chapel:

> What I wanted to do [in St. Benedict Chapel] from the very beginning, first instinctively, then more and more consciously, was this: to make the truth glow. Truth is a power, provided you don't demand an immediate effect but rather have patience and expect that it will take a long time [before you see results]. . . . If anywhere, then here lack of purpose is the greatest power. I have often had that experience. Sometimes, especially in the last years, I had a sense that the truth was standing in space like a living body.[3]

I learned only much later that Guardini's homilies in the chapel were to serve as the first draft of his most popular book, *The Lord.* It doesn't matter, either, that I found him unapproachable, even abrupt in social encounters, somewhat shy, and unwilling to be drawn into anything resembling mere chitchat. What matters is that during those 30 or 40 minutes he gave us the sustenance that nourished us for another week of uncertainty, danger and fear, the strength to face Satan and his demons for another week, and that a mere evocation of his presence at the altar and of his words brought light even into our darkest moments of hopelessness or despair.

When the German armies invaded Poland on September 1, 1939, starting the Second World War, I was spending the final weeks of my six months in the Reich Labor Service in East Prussia, where we were building an airfield in preparation for the invasion of Poland. My mother and some of my Jewish relatives had fled Nazi Germany, others had been or were about to be shipped to concentration camps, and my father had taken up residence in a Benedictine convent south of Berlin. After my discharge from the Labor Service, I returned to Berlin, where my sister also lived, and moved into a furnished room. For the next five years, until Nazi Germany collapsed in the spring of

1945, I worked under Gestapo supervision in various factories and offices designated as "essential to the war effort." The Catholic youth organization New Germany had ceased to exist by decree of the regime. Because my age group was the first to be drafted for the war — I myself being found unworthy to serve because of my half-Jewishness — even clandestine meetings of New Germany no longer took place.

There is no need here to go into any details about the Second World War, except to say that beginning in August 1940, steadily intensifying bombing raids on the city of Berlin became a norm of life that determined how we lived, worked, dressed, felt, behaved — in fact, that made us aware that any day, any hour could be the last of our life.[4] I will spare you the statistics of these bombings. Suffice it to say that Berlin was the most-bombed and most heavily destroyed city of the war.

There is no doubt that the experience of unimaginable terror and destruction marks many of Guardini's books and gives them the singular poignancy of style and unequivocal commitment to truth as he saw it.

Yet we adjusted, as people have the amazing capacity to adjust to almost anything. I can say — and I know the same holds true of countless others — that I never lived as intensely as during those five years during which death or injury were daily, nightly, hourly realities. Guardini, who had been forced to retire from the University of Berlin in 1939, left Berlin in 1943 for Mooshausen, but even though he was spared the nearly total devastation of the city during the last two years of the war, he remained a living presence among us Berliners. There is no doubt that the experience of unimaginable terror and destruction marks many of his books and gives them the singular poignancy of style and unequivocal commitment to truth as he saw it.

In addition to my attendance of his Mass at the Students' Chapel, two events in my life during the war years stand out as particularly illustrative of his influence on our thinking and living. In 1940, I joined what was called the Thomas Circle, a weekly gathering of young men and women in the Catholic Students' Home who, under the guidance of one of the most impressive priests I have ever met, Hermann Joseph Schmidt, systematically studied the *Summa Theologiae* of the "Dumb Sicilian Ox." For the sake of brevity, I have to resist the temptation of giving you examples of how masterfully Hejo, as we called him, brought to life a thirteenth-century vision of the world for people, many of whom wore soldiers' uniforms and were able to attend the meeting only because they were on home leave.

Often, when the sirens began to howl in the middle of our discussions, we had to seek shelter, only to emerge again from the basement to see our street in flames and the walls of our room collapsed and the windows shattered. There was no better opportunity to demonstrate the validity and pertinence of Thomistic philosophy than to test it against the deadly turbulence of those years. And even here Guardini made his presence felt. He was not a systematic theologian, let alone a Thomist, but because most of us had read or were reading one of his books, or had attended his lectures at the university or at the Jesuits' St. Canisius Church, it was inevitable that his name would come up frequently during our discussions if for no other reason than to test his vision against that of St. Thomas and to test the validity of a thirteenth-century theologian against that of a modern philosopher of religion. His books about Dante, Montaigne, Pascal, Dostoevski and Hölderlin were as much part of our discussions as the *Quaestiones disputandae.* Guardini, in short, was an inescapable part of the Thomas Circle, and Hejo handled this exercise in comparative literature brilliantly and unforgettably.

The Thomas Circle ended after less than two years, when the Gestapo arrested Hejo because of his role in the resistance movement and sent him to the Dachau concentration camp. It was a painful, tragic loss for those of us for whom the Thomas Circle had become a center of intellectual and religious formation and mutual support at a time when you could not even speak openly about your views and convictions with fellow parishioners or next-door neighbors.

Fortunately, I found another community that offered me the sustenance I needed to live my life in the factories, offices and furnished rooms of a rapidly disintegrating city. My father, whom the Nazis had forbidden to publish, had become a permanent resident in a small Benedictine convent, the Priory of St. Gertrud, in the countryside some 40 kilometers south of Berlin. The sisters' life centered on the celebration of the eucharist and the praying of the liturgical hours, on the classical Benedictine *Ora et Labora* without compromise.

Because of the uniqueness of their way of life, which was totally devoted to the liturgy and fully open to the popular liturgical renewal flourishing in Germany at that time, they attracted guests from all over Germany for whom the priory, without offering any formal instruction but simply by example, became a center of retreat. From here they returned to their hometowns with a new understanding of how the liturgy can renew and become part not only of their own lives but also of the life of their respective parish communities and religious organizations.

I went to the Priory of St. Gertrud whenever I had a chance to leave Berlin for a few days. It was not only the company of my father — and later of my sister, who also had taken up residence there toward the end of the war — or the participation in the religious life of the sisters that attracted me to the priory. Equally important to me was the fairly stable group of guests who often stayed there for weeks or months and quickly formed a closely knit community of their own. This was not a community as we understand it today; it required that the participants trusted each other in their unequivocal rejection of the Nazi regime, that they were educated and literate, and that conversation was for them not only a means of inspiration and an occasion to exchange views and opinions but above all an indispensable source of support and encouragement.

Because each one of us knew that our very meeting could endanger our lives, these gatherings had a depth of intimacy that I have never again experienced. In a sense, it was the church of the catacombs. Not surprisingly, because the priory had become a center of liturgical renewal — though much less known than, for example, Maria Laach — Guardini was often a central topic of our discussions. As it happened, one of the frequent guests, Ida Maria Soltmann, director of an institution for delinquent girls in Münster and one of the first women in Germany to have received a doctorate, was one of the contributing editors of *Die Schildgenossen,* or Comrades of the Shield, the bi-monthly publication of Quickborn[5] edited by Guardini and the official publication of the Burg Rothenfels movement until the Nazis suppressed it in 1941. I suspect that in some ways she may have been more influential in at least opening up the sisters' liturgical life to the guests and making them fully participate in that life than the two elderly Benedictine monks who were the priory's spiritual directors. Be that as it may, Guardini, again, was ubiquitous.

What I called the reign of Satan and his demons and a Catholic existence resembling that of the times of the persecution by the Romans is the background against which people like Guardini wrote their books and gave their lectures.

I experienced the assault of the Russian armies on Berlin while I was in the priory, and when Germany had surrendered unconditionally, I chose to return to Berlin and become a writer. One of the books I wrote at the time — commissioned by the Catholic Morus Publishing House because I had been a member of a group of the organized Resistance Movement that helped Jews escape into Switzerland — illustrates poignantly that to be a believing, practicing Catholic was for many of us during the Nazi regime not unlike being a believing, practicing Christian during the time of Nero. Entitled *Martyrs of the Diocese of Berlin,* the book contained biographical sketches of 14 men, both priests and lay persons, who had been among the hundreds of priests and thousands of members of the Resistance Movement executed by the Nazis in concentration camps or in prisons because they gave public witness to their conviction that the doctrines and deeds of the Nazi regime stood in radical opposition to what Christians believed and how they were to live their lives.[6] Among these men were three of international renown: Erich Klausener, a director in the Traffic Ministry and leader of the Catholic Action movement; Monsignor Bernhard Lichtenberg, rector of Berlin's St. Hedwig Cathedral; and the Reverend Max Joseph Metzger, founder and leader of the Peace League of German Catholics and an activist in the Una Sancta and Pax Christi movements.

I mention this book not only to show what moved us Catholics during the immediate postwar period but also to express my conviction that what I called the reign of Satan and his demons and a Catholic existence resembling that of the times of the persecution by the Romans is the background against which people like Guardini wrote their books and gave their lectures. One of the most urgent and difficult tasks for writers and teachers in the immediate postwar period, it seems to me, was to reconnect the bond that exists between great European literature and religion and which the collapse of Western culture and civilization, in which the Nazi era was the final chapter that had begun with the First World War, had torn to shreds. How much sense, for example, did a Rilke, a Hermann Hesse, a Pascal, authors who occupied Guardini at that time, still make after the Holocaust or, for that matter, among the ruins of Berlin, Dresden or Cologne? Did they still have a "message" for us, a meaning for people whose homes had been destroyed or who had been driven from their homelands, and who had to build their lives up from the ground, physically, emotionally, intellectually?

It was my good fortune that my last personal encounter with Guardini occurred just at that time, when we had to rediscover the meaning of Western tradition for our time and regain a vision of the world and of religion that was rooted in the inexhaustible treasures of that tradition in art, literature and architecture. In 1947, I decided to enroll at the University of Tübingen to study philosophy, theology and history, but as engaging as these courses turned out to be, my most vivid memories of the year I spent in Tübingen before returning to Berlin to continue my career as a freelance writer were the lectures of Guardini, who held a special chair for Catholic Philosophy of Religion and Weltanschauung at the university. These lectures proved to us that truly great Western literature is fundamentally "religious," anchored in a metaphysical vision of the world that transcends time and circumstances.

Guardini attracted, as usual, a standing-room-only crowd of students and professors of virtually all disciplines and ideological persuasions. This was not because he was a popular teacher in the usual sense; he never was. His innate shyness and a certain disposition to melancholy made him keep his distance from students and colleagues, and he easily became visibly angry about noise or latecomers and interrupted his lectures when he sensed some inattention among the audience. Once, when he noticed that some students had on their lap one or another of his books in which they were reading while he was speaking, he folded up his manuscript and left the room in the middle of the lecture with the words, "Well, if you prefer reading my books instead of listening to what I have to say, I am superfluous here." The incident made the rounds in the university but only added to our fascination with a man who at all times was completely true to himself and never made an attempt to play a role that would enhance his prestige or reputation.

To sum up my most vivid memories of these lectures at Tübingen, it was from them that I gained an understanding of what we would call today Christian existentialism: coming to terms with a secularized world by drawing the strength for daily survival from the Judeo-Christian tradition, from faith, hope, and charity — and beauty — as these are embedded not only in the Christian-oriented masterpieces of that tradition but also in every great work of human creativity. To change the subtitle of our book slightly: We were *re*claiming the sacred in a turbulent world. What Guardini's homilies and eucharistic celebrations in Berlin's St. Benedict Chapel contributed to the formation of my vision of liturgy, my faith and indeed my very survival, his lectures in Tübingen contributed to my understanding of the world in which I lived and in which I had to survive as a Catholic and a writer.

That ends my reflection on these years as far as it concerns my connection with Guardini during an era in European history whose remembrance is for my generation inseparably connected with images of fires in the night. Let me conclude with an observation that extends our concern with "proclaiming the sacred in a modern world" into today's political, social and economic life. After two fratricidal European wars, my generation's most fervent hope was and remains that out of these destructive fires in the night would emerge a United States of Europe founded on and bound together by the beliefs and ethics of Christianity, a modern version, if you will, of the Holy Roman Empire. That, I am sure, was also on the minds of the three men who in 1950 laid the foundation for what is now called the European Union: Konrad Adenauer, then West Germany's Chancellor; Robert Schuman, then French Secretary of State; and Alcide de Gaspari, then Prime Minister of Italy. All three of them were fervent Catholics; their countries bordered on each other, and they were the leaders of their respective Christian Democratic Parties.

When one reads the books Guardini wrote after the Second World War, it is evident that a Europe united in a recognition and acceptance of the Christian vision of the world was also his hope and dream during the last years of his life. In fact, he saw it as the only chance to save what we understand as the Western World. The last sentence of his reflection on *Der Heilbringer* (He Who Brings Salvation), which he wrote in 1946, reads:

> If Europe should still exist in the future, and the world should still need it, then it must remain a historical entity formed by the figure of Christ. . . . If it gives up this nucleus of its identity — whatever remains of Europe doesn't mean much any more.[7]

Still, Guardini, unlike some of our best thinkers, also believed that a Europe united in Christ was possible. In his book *Power and Responsibility,* which appeared in German in 1951, he expressed his conviction of a positive solution, a solution that ultimately depended on the responsibility of the free person before God. "I therefore believe," he wrote, "that only this freedom has a chance to lead history along a positive road."[8]

"Proclaiming the sacred in a modern world" (to quote our book's subtitle), then, is the personal daily, hourly responsibility of each of us, no matter what our vocation as believers. That is Guardini's legacy, a legacy that ranks him as one of those truly classic Catholic writers whose thinking and vision are as pertinent to our own chaotic times as they were 40 years ago when he saw in the ruins of Europe the unmistakable signs of hope.

Endnotes

1. Romano Guardini, *Das Ende der Neuzeit. Ein Versuch zur Orientierung/Die Macht. Versuch einer Wegweisung* (Mainz: Matthias Grünewald, 1986; Paderborn: Ferdinand Schöningh, 1986), 77. These two books are published in one volume. The books in English are *The End of the Modern World,* trans. J. Theman and H. Burke (New York: Sheed and Ward, 1956), 111 – 12, and *Power and Responsibility,* trans. Elinor C. Briefs (Chicago: Henry Regnery Company, 1961). Translations from the German in this chapter are by H. Kuehn.

2. Guardini, *Das Ende der Neuzeit,* 24. See idem, *The End of the Modern World,* 37.

3. Romano Guardini, *Berichte über mein Leben: Autobiographische Aufzeichnungen* (Düsseldorf: Patmos, 1985), 109 – 10.

4. See Heinz R. Kuehn, *Mixed Blessings: An Almost Ordinary Life in Hitler's Germany* (Athens, Georgia: University of Georgia Press, 1989).

5. The Quickborn ("wellspring of life") was a Catholic youth association that existed from 1909 until 1939. Its national center was Burg Rothenfels am Main near Würzburg.

6. Heinz R. Kühn, *Blutzeugen des Bistums Berlin* (Berlin: Morus Verlag, 1951).

7. Romano Guardini, *Der Heilbringer in Mythos, Offenbarung, und Politik* (Mainz: Matthias Grünewald, 1979), 81.

8. Guardini, *Die Macht,* 154; idem, *Power and Responsibility,* 66.

Chapter Two

A Precursor's Life and Work

Robert A. Krieg, CSC

On April 28, 1962, European dignitaries, bishops and intellectual leaders gathered in Brussels, the city at Western Europe's geographical center, and witnessed the conferral of the prestigious Erasmus Prize by Prince H. Bernhard of the Netherlands upon a man who was himself a living center of European thought and culture: Romano Guardini.

Established four years earlier, the Erasmus Prize of the Amsterdam-based European Foundation of Culture bestows international recognition upon "individuals or institutions who have made important contributions to European culture in respect of culture, social sciences or social questions."[1] Previously it had been awarded to president of Austria Adolf Schärf (1958), the philosopher Karl Jaspers and the French statesman Robert Schuman (1959), and the painters Marc Chagall and Oskar Kokoschka (1960). The year after Guardini's honor, it was awarded to the Jewish philosopher Martin Buber (1963). Twenty years later it was conferred upon the theologian Edward Schillebeeckx, OP (1982). In awarding the prize to Romano Guardini in 1962, the Erasmus Foundation singled out Guardini as a humanist, as an individual who had brought together and given new direction to Europe's rich, centuries-old heritage of respect for the dignity and promise of human life.

Today the name Romano Guardini is unfamiliar to most people under the age of 40, but for those over 40 it can bring back memories of their awakening to the renewal of American Catholicism in the 1950s and 1960s. Moreover, mention of the life and work of this inspiring writer can help both young and old see more clearly where we have come from and where we are headed. For this reason it is currently worthwhile to ask, who was this now somewhat forgotten priest-scholar, and what did he write?

Karl Rahner's Portrait of Romano Guardini

The renowned theologian Karl Rahner gave an illuminating sketch of Romano Guardini on the occasion of his death on October 1, 1968. Rahner points out that Guardini was born into a Catholic church that saw itself "as an intellectually, culturally and humanly self-sufficient, closed society, on the defensive, seeking to win support by her conservatism." But during his last years, Guardini saw the church assume a new stance toward the world through the decisions of the Second Vatican Council. This renewed church is one that "plunges into the situation of the time, giving and also ready to receive, sharing the problems and the perils of the time, bursting into a new age which even it cannot plan in advance, serving and concerned not with itself but with men [and women]." In Rahner's judgment, Guardini deserves some of the credit for the church's new, open stance toward the modern world. Referring to Guardini, Rahner writes: "In the many-sidedness of his work, he might well be regarded as the very first of the German-speaking contributors to this *aggiornamento*."[2]

In Rahner's judgment, Guardini deserves some of the credit for the church's new, open stance toward the modern world.

According to Rahner, Romano Guardini was a "religious visionary" who called attention to the Holy Spirit's new stirrings within the Catholic church. Moreover, he was an interpreter both of scripture, whose words express the living word of God, and also of great literary works, like those of Plato, Fyodor Dostoevski and Rainer Maria Rilke, which offer profound insights into human life and our quest for God. At the same time, Guardini was a creative theologian who, breaking away from neoscholasticism, renewed our understanding of the liturgy, the church and Jesus Christ. Rahner holds that when one considers "the really unique character of his work," one sees that Guardini's writing "was meant to serve only the eternal in man, his original and authentic relationship to God, as it is lived and not merely talked about. All this in countless pages telling of man and thus seeking to tell of God, who is the true mystery of man." Finally, it is important to add, Rahner says, that within a church marked by a "ghetto Catholicism," Romano Guardini was one of the foremost proponents of "cultural Catholicism," of a Catholicism committed to the pursuit of truth in the culture of the day as well as in scripture and the Judeo-Christian tradition.[3]

In his eulogy, Karl Rahner conveyed a great deal in few words. He provided a glimpse of a complex, creative person and his contribution to twentieth-century Catholicism, and left it to others to paint fuller portraits of Guardini.[4] Such is the aim of this second chapter. In the following pages we will review the four major phases of Guardini's 83 years of life: his youth from 1885 to 1906, his student years from 1906 to 1923, his professorship in Berlin from 1923 to 1945, and his professorship in Tübingen and Munich from 1945 until his death in 1968.[5] Expanding on Rahner's eulogy, this chapter portrays Romano Guardini as a forerunner of the Second Vatican Council.[6]

Youth: The Mainz Years, 1885–1906

Romano Michele Antonio Maria Guardini had the good fortune of being born in Verona, Italy, and growing up in Mainz, Germany, both of which are cities steeped in the humanism of Western civilization. Born on February 17, 1885, he spent his first months in his parents' apartment not far from Verona's Roman amphitheater, built in the first century after Christ. The statue of Dante Alighieri (d. 1321), who was protected in Verona by Cangrande I, stands in a plaza at the heart of the city — the city of Shakespeare's tragedy of Romeo and Juliet. Across the Adige River, there is situated the Giusti Gardens, where Johann Wolfgang Goethe (d. 1832) found inspiration for many of his writings. While Romano himself was too young, of course, to be aware of his rich surroundings, his parents were deeply conscious of them, as evidenced by the fact that his father gave him, at an early age, a leather-bound copy of Dante's *Divine Comedy*. This book, with its profound narrative of the poet's journey through hell, purgatory and heaven, remained close to Romano until the end of his life.

During his first year, Romano moved with his parents to Mainz, which stands at the confluence of the Rhine River as it flows from the Alps to the North Sea and the Main River, which joins the Rhine after having made its way westward from central Germany. This point of intersection of north-south and east-west commerce was important to Romano's father, who imported poultry and eggs from Italy. (In 1910 his father became a member of the Italian consulate in Germany.) This location was also crucial in the young Guardini's life because he grew up influenced by the expressions of Western culture that he saw when he visited Mainz's museums with their ancient artifacts of the Teutons and Romans, the city's Roman fortress overlooking the Rhine and Main rivers, and its churches from seventh century. He was also aware at an early age that Mainz was the home of Johann Gutenberg (d. 1468), who invented the first printing press with movable type — the press that made it possible to distribute Martin Luther's Bible throughout the German-speaking world during the Reformation. This rich mixture of European history and culture nurtured the soul of Romano, as evidenced in his early essay "Thule and Hellas" (1928).[7]

In their home, Romano and his younger brothers—Gino, Mario and Aleardo—were introduced by their parents, Romano Tullo and Paola Maria, to the world south of the Alps. The family spoke Italian among themselves, stayed in contact with their relatives in Italy, and on occasion traveled to Verona for a holiday. Moreover, they retained their Italian citizenship, for both parents were ardent Italian nationalists who intended to return to Verona. In fact, soon after Romano Tullo's death in 1919, Paola Maria (d. 1957) left Mainz and moved to Lake Como and eventually to her family estate at Isola Vincentina, not far from Verona.

At school in Mainz, the young Romano was educated within the West's humanistic heritage. Already fluent in German and Italian, he also learned Latin, Greek, French and English. Along with his classmates, he studied the classic texts of Western civilization. From the outset, he exhibited enthusiasm and exceptional talent in his studies. He read texts by Dante, Shakespeare and Stendahl in their original languages. As he was finishing high school at the Rabanus Maurus Gymnasium, he was invited to join with a handful of other gifted students in frequent discussions on history, the arts and religious belief at the home of Dr. Wilhelm Schleussner and Frau Josephine Schleussner, a childless married couple who for many years sponsored a study circle to nurture the intellectual interests of Mainz's most talented Catholic youth.

Soon after his graduation from the gymnasium on August 7, 1903, Romano Guardini entered into what would become one of the most traumatic periods of his life. From October 1903 until July 1904, he studied chemistry at the University of Tübingen. No matter how hard he worked, however, he could not understand his courses' subject matter and, as a result, received low grades. Moreover, this experience of failure fed into Guardini's melancholic disposition, and he found himself engulfed by depression and loneliness. At the end of the 1903–1904 academic year, Guardini withdrew from the study of chemistry in Tübingen and decided to switch to the study of economics at the University of Munich. Although he fared better in economics, he did not enjoy his studies and continued to struggle with despondency. Furthermore, as he saw that many of his university peers had abandoned their Christian faith, he questioned his own beliefs. It is noteworthy that amid his confusion he discovered one continual source of delight and intellectual excitement: Munich's concerts, theaters and museums.

At the end of the 1904–1905 academic year, Guardini returned to his family's home on Gonsenheimer Strasse in Mainz and found himself in a crisis of faith. After numerous discussions with his childhood friend Karl Neundörfer, Guardini underwent a moving experience, which he later compared to Augustine's conversion. One afternoon in his attic room, he discovered the truth of Matthew 10:39: "Those who find their life will lose it; those who lose their life for my sake will find it." For the remainder of his life, Guardini frequently spoke on the leap of faith that is required for the Christian life.

The resolution of Guardini's crisis of faith laid the foundation for his next decision. In the autumn of 1905, Guardini went to Berlin to resume his courses in economics and again found himself dissatisfied with his studies and burdened with depression. Then one morning as he prayed in the Dominican Paulus Kirche, it dawned on him that his deepest desire was to study theology and be ordained to the priesthood. A few weeks later, after a series of meetings with a priest, he decided to change his course of studies for a third time.

A Young Scholar: The University Years, 1906–1923

Romano Guardini began his theological studies in March 1906 at the University of Freiburg im Breisgau. This transition initially was so hard that he nearly "drowned" in waves of depression, and at one point he even thought of suicide. Nevertheless, he became increasingly enthusiastic about his studies. After one semester, he moved to the University of Tübingen to benefit from the institution's rich theological tradition. Here, for the next three semesters, he was deeply influenced by the open-minded approach to theology of the priest-scholar Wilhelm Koch, who beginning in 1907 was accused of Modernism and was eventually forced to resign from the faculty.

Residing at Tübingen's seminary, the Wilhelmsstift, Guardini and a few friends, including Karl Neundörfer and Josef Weiger, formed a study circle, which they called the Schönfurzia. In this informal group they discussed literature, the arts and their own writings. One fruit of this activity was Guardini's first publication, an essay titled "Michelangelo: Poems and Letters" (1907). At the initiative of Weiger, Guardini visited the nearby Abbey of Beuron and was immediately drawn to the liturgical celebrations of the Benedictine monks, who were in the forefront of the liturgical renewal. After many retreats at the Abbey, he eventually became an Oblate of St. Benedict, taking the name Odilio.

In October 1908, Guardini and Neundörfer entered the seminary for the diocese of Mainz, in the shadow of Mainz's cathedral. Here, they were instructed in neo-scholasticism, which after their studies at the University of Tübingen appeared arid, ahistorical and intellectually stifling. When they voiced their dissatisfaction with their studies to seminary officials, they were immediately suspected of Modernism and required

19

to postpone their ordinations for six months. On May 28, 1910, Romano Guardini was ordained by Bishop Georg Heinrich Kirstein; on the next day, he celebrated Mass with his parents' gifts, a chalice and paten crafted at the Abbey of Beuron.

During the next two years, Guardini served at a parish in Heppenheim, at a hospital in Darmstadt, at the Cathedral of Worms and at Mainz's St. Christopher Church. Because he also desired to teach religion and could not do so without German citizenship, he made a decision that his parents opposed: On August 8, 1911, he became a German citizen. At work, too, in this decision was Guardini's awareness that, having lived twenty-five of his twenty-six years in Germany, he had become German in spirit. In his words: "While I spoke and thought in Italian at home, I grew up intellectually in the German language and culture. . . . I felt that I belonged interiorly to the German essence."[8]

Guardini visited the nearby Abbey of Beuron and was immediately drawn to the liturgical celebrations of the Benedictine monks, who were in the forefront of the liturgical renewal.

From the outset, it was clear to both Guardini and diocesan officials that the young priest should pursue further studies. Hence, in October 1912, Guardini commenced his doctoral studies in theology at the University of Freiburg im Breisgau with the understanding that he would return to his diocese and eventually teach theology in the seminary. When it came time to choose a dissertation topic, he showed his independence by deciding to write not on St. Thomas Aquinas under the direction of Carl Braig, which would have satisfied the neoscholastic professors at Mainz's seminary, but on St. Bonaventure, whose neo-Platonic thought was congenial to him. Directed by Engelbert Krebs, Guardini wrote a thesis on "The Teaching of St. Bonaventure on Salvation" and was awarded his PHD on May 15, 1915.

Returning to the diocese of Mainz, he was assigned during the next five years to work within Mainz itself at St. Ignatius Church, St. Emmeran Church and St. Peter Church. Simultaneously, he served as the chaplain to the diocesan youth group called Iuventus. Drawing on his experience in the Schleussners' study circle and in the Schönfurzia at the Wilhelmsstift, he broadened the activities of Iuventus to include discussions of literature, theater and art as well as retreats and social events. Moreover, with Germany locked into the Great War, Guardini fulfilled his military duty by working part-time as a hospital orderly from the autumn of 1916 until the spring of 1918. (Hence, he had already completed his military service when Germany surrendered in November 1918 and Wilhelm II abdicated the throne.) Somehow, amid all of these responsibilities,

Guardini also made time to work on a manuscript concerning the principles of authentic worship. When he finished the text in 1918, he showed it to Abbot Ildefons Herwegen at Maria Laach Abbey, who immediately published the book whose title in English is *The Spirit of the Liturgy*. Soon afterwards, this short work was a best-seller throughout Germany.

In light of the success of *The Spirit of the Liturgy*, Guardini decided to write a Habilitationsschrift (scholarly monograph), which is required in Germany for university teaching. With permission from the diocese of Mainz, Guardini moved to the University of Bonn in the autumn of 1920. As he engaged in further theological studies under the direction of Gerhard Esser, he also entered into discussions and correspondence with the Jewish philosopher Martin Buber, the phenomenologist Max Scheler and the art historian Paul Clemen. At the same time, he became increasingly active in the rapidly growing Catholic youth movement, in particular in the Quickborn ("the wellspring of life"), whose national center was located at Burg Rothenfels am Main, not far from Würzburg.

In the spring of 1922 Guardini completed his Habilitationsschrift concerning St. Bonaventure's teaching on the illumination of the mind. A few months later, he gave a series of lectures on the nature of the church at the national conference of the Catholic Academic Association. These lectures were so well received that in early 1923 they appeared as the book *The Church and the Catholic*. They also resulted in Guardini's receiving two academic "calls." The University of Bonn offered Guardini the chair of Practical Theology and Liturgical Studies, which he declined because he did not want to become an academic specialist. Soon afterwards, in the winter of 1923, he was invited to the newly established chair of Philosophy of Religion and Catholic Weltanschauung (worldview) at the University of Berlin, which he accepted. In the spring of 1923, as the Weimar Republic staggered under soaring inflation, Guardini moved to Germany's national capital.

This move marked the second major transition in Guardini's life, for with it he virtually severed his ties to the diocese of Mainz. Since his mother and brothers had returned to Italy in 1919, he no longer had family in Mainz. Also, he was now certain that he would never be allowed to teach at Mainz's seminary, and at the time no university existed in Mainz. Having left Mainz in 1920, Guardini would not visit there until 1943.[9]

The Young Professor: The Berlin Years, 1923–1945

The young Guardini (38 years old) did not feel warmly welcomed to Germany's prestigious Friedrich Wilhelm University in Berlin, since 1949 named Humbolt University. Catholics were a minority in Berlin, and many members of the university's predominantly Protestant faculty still remembered the Kulturkampf (1871–1880). Furthermore, the faculty of theology was entirely Protestant. As a result, Guardini had to receive his appointment from the department of Catholic theology at the University of Breslau. Berlin's theological faculty had resisted the effort to establish a chair for a Catholic theologian but had to yield to pressure from the Weimar government, which depended on the political support of the Catholic Center Party. This resistance concretely manifested itself during Guardini's first weeks in Berlin, when the university's receptionist would answer queries about the new professor by saying that there was no Professor Guardini at the university. But Guardini overcame this animosity. He soon won over professors as well as students by his engaging, insightful lectures. He became so highly respected that he managed to retain his academic chair for the next twenty years, the first ten years during the Weimar Republic and the second ten years during the Third Reich.[10]

In the lecture hall and in his writings, Guardini blossomed as a Renaissance person, a humanistic scholar with interdisciplinary pursuits and no narrow academic specialty. He taught three types of courses: systematic theology, divine revelation in the New Testament, and religion and literature. He attracted such large crowds of students, professors and interested listeners that his lecture halls were always filled to overflowing. Among those who heard Guardini speak were Hannah Arendt and Hans Urs von Balthasar, as well as Heinz R. Kuehn (see chapter 1) and Regina Kuehn (see chapter 7). It was from these lectures that Guardini wrote some of his books, for example, on Anselm of Canterbury (1923), the theory of opposites (*Der Gegensatz,* 1925), Pascal (1935), Augustine (1935), Dostoevski (1939) and Socrates (1943). Sadly, since his work did not rely on the categories and language of neoscholasticism, Guardini's writings were initially dismissed by many Catholic bishops and theologians.

Guardini's success in communicating with Germany's young people was not confined to the lecture hall. The young scholar held weekly informal discussions on art, literature and religion. Furthermore, he was active in pastoral ministry. Beginning in 1924, he presided at the eucharist in chapel of the Soziale Fraue Schule on Wednesdays, and starting in 1928 he presided at the eucharist on Sundays at St. Benedict Chapel on Schlüterstrasse. (Here he was introduced to Heinz and Regina Kuehn.) His preaching and spiritual conferences eventually served as the basis for some of his writings, including *Letters from*

Lake Como (1927), *Sacred Signs* (1929), *The Living God* (1929) and *The Life of Faith* (1935). Also, Guardini's meditations "on the life of the Lord," which he offered at St. Benedict Chapel and in spiritual conferences at Burg Rothenfels during Adolf Hitler's first years as Germany's "Führer," appeared as the book *The Lord* in 1937. To its German readers the book's message was in part implicitly political: Despite the Nazi greeting *"Heil Hitler!"* ("Salvation in Hitler!"), there is only one bearer of salvation *("Heil"),* Jesus Christ.

The Reich stripped Guardini of his professional and pastoral involvements, thereby treating him as a non-person, an individual with no status within the public realm.

In 1923 Guardini assumed leadership of the Quickborn. In the following year, he also took charge of the Quickborn's journal *Die Schildgenossen,* which then quickly evolved into a national Catholic periodical devoted to theology and culture. He insisted that the Quickborn promote the cultural life of youth as well as their spiritual and social dimensions. As a result, at the Quickborn's local and national gatherings young people discussed theater, art and literature, played musical instruments, and joined in retreats and pilgrimages to holy shrines. At Burg Rothenfels young men and women from all corners of Germany learned folk dances and folk songs, acted in the plays of Shakespeare, and even performed puppet shows. They also participated in informal Masses at which they sang hymns in German instead of Latin, discussed the scriptural readings for the day, and stood around an altar at which the priest faced the people. Further, they were introduced to Guardini's vision of a "new Europe" that would transcend national and ethnic boundaries and be founded on the West's tradition of humanism.

Tragically, Guardini's world was destroyed in 1939. On March 11, the Nazis dismissed Guardini from the University of Berlin, and on August 7, Hitler's SS seized the Quickborn's castle at Rothenfels. As it disbanded all Catholic youth organizations, it coerced young Catholics throughout Germany to join the Hitler Youth Association. Subsequently, in 1941, the Reich banned even *Die Schildgenossen.* In short, the Reich stripped Guardini of his professional and pastoral involvements, thereby treating him as a non-person, an individual with no status within the public realm.

In this vacuum, Guardini turned to his writing and quickly completed manuscripts on which he had been working. These included *The World and the Person* (1939), *The Rosary* (1940), his book on divine revelation, *Die Offenbarung* (1940), *The Death of Socrates* (1943) and *Prayer in Practice* (1943), which is also titled *The Art of Praying.* Without any formal academic appointments, Guardini also gave lectures at Berlin's Catholic *Volkshochschule,* offered evening classes at the Jesuit St. Canisius Church and, by presiding at Masses at St. Benedict Chapel, continued to serve as a spiritual leader for Catholics in a city that was increasingly, day and night, the target of Allied bombers.

By the summer of 1943, Guardini found himself in the third major transition of his life. Like his earlier turning points, this one too resulted in a geographical change. After the Reich advised German citizens to move away from Berlin if they were able to do so, Guardini — weary from the incessant bombing — packed some of his belongings (with the help of Regina Kuehn) and moved to the rural parish of St. John the Baptist in Mooshausen, in the Allgäu region of southern Germany. Here, residing with his friend Pastor Josef Weiger, he remained until the end of the war. As he approached his 60th birthday on February 17, 1945, he wrote his autobiographical reflections, which were published posthumously in 1984 under the title *Berichte über mein Leben* (Reports About My Life). As Guardini awaited the outcome of the war, he had no idea what the future held for him.

The Mature Professor: The Munich Years, 1945 – 1968

In the postwar years, Romano Guardini emerged as a national voice of hope. In a variety of settings, he proclaimed a humanistic vision of a new Germany within a united Europe.

In autumn 1945, he moved to the University of Tübingen to serve as Professor of Philosophy of Religion and Christian Weltanschauung. Here he remained for two years, turning down "calls" to the universities of Göttingen, Munich and Freiburg im Breisgau, where he was offered Martin Heidegger's chair. Then, in 1948, he accepted the invitation to the University of Munich. Assuming the specially created chair of Philosophy of Religion and Christian Weltanschauung within the faculty of philosophy, he remained in this academic position until 1963, when he was succeeded by Karl Rahner. As in Berlin, Guardini filled the lecture halls of Tübingen and Munich with students, professors and international guests. (Some of these events in Munich were attended by Albert K. Wimmer and Thomas F. O'Meara; see chapter 7.)

During these years, Guardini was influential outside the lecture hall as well as within it. He offered advice concerning the new direction of the German press, radio and television to former members of the Quickborn such as Walter Dirks, the editor of the *Frankfurter Hefte,* and Clemens Münster, cultural director of Radio Munich. In 1948 he gave a lecture on peace in France, thereby becoming one of the first German citizens to give a public lecture in France after the war. Along with Germany's chancellor, Konrad Adenauer, Guardini publicly declared that, in light of the Holocaust, Germans had a moral responsibility to pay reparations to the Jewish people. Moreover, every Sunday during the academic year in Munich he preached to overflowing congregations at the university's St. Ludwig Church. (After one of these Masses, he met his longtime friends Dr. Franz Mueller and Dr. Therese Mueller with their daughter Gertrud; see chapters 7 and 8.)

At the same time, Guardini continued to be a prolific writer. During these years, he wrote, for instance, *The End of the Modern Age* (1950), *Power and Responsibility* (1951), *Rilke's Duino Elegies* (1953) and *The Virtues* (1963). At the request of the German bishops, he provided a new translation of the psalms, entitled *Deutscher Psalter* (1950), and subsequently he wrote *Meditations Before Mass* (1955), *The Wisdom of the Psalms* (1963) and *The Church of the Lord* (1965). Moreover, he made further contributions to the renewal of the liturgy, for example, by presenting his essay "The Liturgy and the Spiritual Situation of Our Age" at the First German Liturgical Congress (Frankfurt am Main) in 1950. And in 1964, at the age of 79, he sent his thought-provoking letter on "the cultic-act and the present challenge facing liturgical education" to the Third German Liturgical Congress (Mainz).[11]

During his last years, Guardini experienced what may be described as the fourth major transition of his life. In his "theological letters to a friend," namely Josef Weiger, he disclosed that he was rethinking his theology. He explained that he found himself shifting his attention from Jesus Christ, who was the center point of his thought since his youth, to the God of Jesus Christ. In particular, he found himself reflecting anew upon the goodness of creation and the issues of evil and human suffering.[12] In this vein, as he was dying he mentioned to Walter Dirks that he awaited the moment when he could ask God about the absurd suffering of innocent victims in history.[13] Throughout his life and even in his dying, Romano Guardini remained a religious wayfarer, one in search of the truth and not afraid to ask fresh questions of himself, of the world and of God.

A Precursor of Vatican II

As Karl Rahner recalled in his eulogy for Romano Guardini, this humanist scholar died in a church that was quite different from the church into which he was born. The church of Vatican I saw itself as a fortress or bastion of truth against the errors of the Enlightenment; in contrast, the church of Vatican II sees itself as a pilgrim people on its way, in dialogue with other peoples, to the reign of God. This drastic shift in ecclesial self-understanding came to full public recognition in the mid-1960s with the Council's adoption of *Lumen Gentium* (*The Dogmatic Constitution on the Church,* 1964) and

Gaudium et Spes (*The Pastoral Constitution on the Church in the Modern World,* 1965), but it was actually occurring throughout the late 1800s and early 1900s — hence throughout the course of Guardini's life. And, as Rahner has pointed out, Guardini was one of the earliest proponents of this new, or more accurately, this renewed understanding of the church's nature and mission. Throughout his life, he had advocated ecclesial and liturgical renewal not only in his writings but also in his very activities.

Guardini's writings prepared the way for the Second Vatican Council by both their content and their form. According to Guardini, the heart or "essence" of the church is not a collection of dogmas and regulations but a person, Jesus Christ alive in the Holy Spirit. Or, as Vatican II said, the living Christ is the reality to whom the church witnesses, the reality of which the church is sacrament. Furthermore, Guardini held that the church is primarily not an institution but a community, the assembly of people united by the Holy Spirit with Jesus Christ and in Christ with one another. This Pauline understanding of the body of Christ is conveyed in Vatican II's view of the church as the people of God, the pilgrim people, and today this conciliar ecclesiology is expressed in the notion of the church as *communio*.[14] Also, in Guardini's judgment, on the one hand the fullness of God's revelation is manifest in Jesus Christ, and yet on the other hand God's grace is at work throughout all of creation. Or, in the language of Vatican II, the church finds God's truth in divine revelation as known within scripture and tradition, and yet the church also recognizes that other religions too may share to varying degrees in divine revelation.

The form of Guardini's writings also gained acceptance in the documents of the Second Vatican Council. Guardini began his theological reflections not on the basis of the conventional, specialized issues and topics within Catholic theology but on the basis of the fundamental concerns and questions which were on the minds and hearts of his listeners in specific situations. Then he spoke to these topics not by means of the categories and technical terms of neoscholasticism but rather within a language of personalism that was concrete and rich in metaphors. So, too, Vatican II took as its starting point not the unaddressed topics of Vatican I but the urgent, underlying issues and ideas that emerged from the local churches as expressed by the bishops and *periti.* Moreover, the council spoke to these topics within an ordinary discourse, not a highly philosophical or theological language, that relies not on flat definitions and abstract concepts but on images, straightforward distinctions and accessible analogies. Just as Guardini wrote his articles and books for the variety of men and women who came to his lectures, so too Vatican II crafted its documents for the Catholic community at large.

Guardini cleared a path to the Second Vatican Council not only by his writings but also by his very life. He worked outside the church in the secular universities of Berlin, Tübingen and Munich. He interacted with young people within settings such as Burg Rothenfels that put them at ease and invited their honesty. Also, he entered into dialogue with artists and scholars both in person and by means of their works, and he took seriously new forms of communication, for example, film, radio and television. At the same time, he cherished the long-established forms of the theater, concert hall and museum. In all of his relationships, activities and involvements, Guardini exhibited the kind of orientation espoused by Vatican II in *The Pastoral Constitution on the Church in the Modern World.*

Guardini's close ties with the Second Vatican Council are further evidenced by the fact that in 1961 he was named by Pope John XXIII to serve on the council's preparatory commission on the liturgy. In 1968, when news of Guardini's death reached a meeting of the post-conciliar commission to implement Vatican II's *Constitution on the Sacred Liturgy,* the commission's thirty bishops and their advisors stood and sang the *De Profundis.*[15]

By the time of his death at age 83, Guardini's writings and life had made a profound impact on Catholics around the world. He had written at least sixty books and more than one hundred articles, and many of these publications had been translated into at least three or four languages. Furthermore, in the course of his forty years of teaching and preaching, he had lectured to thousands of spellbound listeners who to this day can remember some of the things Guardini said and how he appeared standing behind his lectern.

Guardini's positive influence on people, the church and society is reflected in the awards and recognition he received in his later years. In 1952 he was named a papal prelate by Pope Pius XII, and in that same year he was the recipient of the Peace Prize of the German Booksellers Association. He was honored in 1955 with Munich's Gold Medal of Honor, and in 1959 with the Great Cross of Merit of the Bundes Republic of Germany. As already mentioned, in 1962 he received the Erasmus Prize. In 1958 he was received into the Bavarian Order of Merit and also into the Peace Association of the Order "Pour le mérite." The city of his birth, Verona, conferred the San Zeno Award on its honored son in 1963. In 1965 he was awarded the German Cross of Merit with Star and Munich's Golden Medallion of Honor. He also received honorary doctorates from the University of Padua (1965) and the University of Bologna (1969).[16] Moreover, shortly

This portrait of Guardini, wearing his academic robes for the philosophy faculty of the University of Munich, was taken in 1960, when he was 75 years old.

before his death, Guardini was offered the cardinal's hat by Pope Paul VI, but he respectfully declined the honor.

Much of Guardini's life and work was summed up when he was awarded the Erasmus Prize. This prestigious honor acknowledged that Romano Guardini made a lasting contribution to the tradition of humanism. By his writings and work he had strengthened and given direction to the West's cherished ideals, including the dignity of human life, respect for all persons, the primacy of truth, the life of the mind and the promise of an international community. Moreover, the Erasmus Award implicitly acknowledged that in Romano Guardini, the Catholic church had come out of its fortress and entered the twentieth century. Just as the election of John F. Kennedy as president of the United States in 1960 symbolized the coming of age of Catholics in North America, the conferring of the Erasmus Prize upon Romano Guardini manifested that Catholics had become full participants in the cultural and intellectual life of modern Europe. The Erasmus Prize made clear that Romano Guardini was a foremost representative of "cultural Catholicism," of the "church in the modern world."

Today, Romano Guardini is buried in a small cemetery beside St. Laurentius Church in Munich. Near him are the graves of other priests who formed with him an Oratorian community in Munich during Guardini's last years. On Guardini's memorial stone is carved the inscription fashioned by the theologian himself:

Romano Guardini
Born in Verona, 17 February 1885
Died in Munich, 1 October 1968
Believing in Jesus Christ and his Church
Trusting in his merciful judgment

Endnotes

1. This sentence from the Erasmus Prize itself is quoted in John Bowden, *Edward Schillebeeckx* (New York: Crossroad, 1983), 36.

2. Karl Rahner, "Thinker and Christian, Obituary of Romano Guardini," in idem, *Opportunities for Faith,* trans. by Edward Quinn (New York: Seabury, 1975), 127–31.

3. As Rahner notes, this characterization of Guardini is given by G. Maron, "Guardini, Romano," in *Die Religion Geschichte und Gegenwart* 2 (1958), 1900.

4. In an interview shortly before his death in 1984, Rahner said that Romano Guardini was "primarily a philosopher of religion, one who describes religious phenomenon with great insight and patience." See Karl Rahner, *I Remember,* trans. Harvey D. Egan (New York: Crossroad 1985), 73–75.

5. The biographical sketch in the remainder of this chapter is primarily derived from Romano Guardini, *Berichte über mein Leben,* ed. Franz Henrich (Düsseldorf: Patmos, 1984) and Hanna-Barbara Gerl, *Romano Guardini 1885–1968* (Mainz: Matthias Grünewald, 1985). Gerl singles out 1915, when he received his PH.D., as a transitional year for Guardini (p. 90). Without denying the importance of this moment, I see it fitting into the second phase of Guardini's life. I agree too with Gerl when she speaks of 1939, with the loss of his professorship, as the beginning of a shift in Guardini's life (p. 317).

6. This view of R. Guardini is also held by Paul Misner, "Guardini, Romano," in the *New Catholic Encyclopedia,* vol. 16: *Supplement 1967–1974* (1974), 198.

7. For complete information concerning R. Guardini's publications, see Hans Mercker with the Katholische Akademie in Bayern (eds.), *Bibliographie Romano Guardini 1885-1968* (Paderborn: Ferdinand Schöningh, 1978).

8. Romano Guardini, "'Europa' und 'Christliche Weltanschauung'" (1955), in idem, *Stationen und Rückblicke* (Würzburg: Werkbund, 1965), 13. Editor's note: Unless otherwise noted, this chapter's translations from the German are by R. Krieg.

9. Nevertheless, Guardini felt lifelong ties to Mainz. See Guardini, *Berichte,* p. 15, and "Romano Guardini," *Wahrheit des Denkens und Wahrheit des Tuns* (Paderborn: Ferdinand Schöningh, 1980), 114.

10. See Gerl, *Romano Guardini,* 279.

11. Romano Guardini, "A Letter from Romano Guardini," *Herder Correspondence* 1 (Special Issue 1964): 24–26.

12. Romano Guardini, *Theologische Briefe an einem Freund* (Paderborn: Ferdinand Schöningh, 1976).

13. Quoted in Karl Rahner, "Why Does God Allow Us to Suffer?" in idem, *Theological Investigations,* vol. 19: *Faith and Ministry,* trans. Edward Quinn (New York: Crossroad, 1983), 207–208.

14. Walter Kasper, "The Church as Communion" (1986), in idem, *Theology and Church,* trans. Margaret Kohl (New York: Crossroad, 1989), 148–165.

15. Regina Kuehn, "Romano Guardini: The Teacher of Teachers" in Robert L. Tuzik (ed.), *How Firm A Foundation: Leaders of the Liturgical Movement* (Chicago: Liturgy Training Publications, 1990), 36–49, 36. See the eleventh plenary session of the Concilium ad Exequendam Constitution de S. Liturgia, October 6, 1968.

16. This list of honors is taken from Mercker, *Bibliographie,* 466.

Chapter Three

The Major Theological Themes of Romano Guardini

Arno Schilson

Whoever wishes to speak about the theology of Romano Guardini faces a difficulty: Guardini was not a theologian in the narrow sense of the word. He himself did not want to be considered a representative of the theology of his day.[1] He even refused several invitations to become a professor of theology. But despite his refusal of a specifically theological role within the university, this scholar made a significant impact upon theology.

His unique way of reflecting upon the Christian faith became ground-breaking for Catholic theology both prior to Vatican II and afterwards. Through his writings and his influence both inside and outside the academy, Guardini decisively contributed in such a way that the church and theology have opened themselves to the world and no longer ignore the challenges of the twentieth century. Therefore, it is still rewarding today to reflect upon the "theological themes" of this "non-theologian." Clearly, in his day Guardini understood better than those in the theological guild how to pursue the craft of theology.

The Theological Work of a "Non-theologian"

The degree to which Guardini as a philosopher of religion engaged in theology becomes evident when we look at his "many books."[2]

Two texts by Guardini that have not received much attention are his early academic books, namely his dissertation of 1915 and his Habilitationsschrift of 1921–1922. Both works treat the theology of St. Bonaventure and are of considerable importance for understanding Guardini's later thought. The first work lays out Bonaventure's soteriology, while the second work shows the "system-forming elements" of his theology. Both studies call attention to the kind of theology that Guardini himself favored.[3] Thus — to mention only a few aspects — these studies stress the uniting of theory and practical reflections. Also, in place of the analytical and abstract form of the scholasticism derived from Thomas Aquinas, Guardini gave prominence to Bonaventure's approach to concrete reality. He highlighted the Franciscan's synthetic, that is, organic method, which brings together many diverse elements. Moreover, Guardini stressed this theology's "movement toward the mystical." These aspects also became important in Guardini's thought.

In contrast to these early works, Guardini's numerous, subsequent publications have received much attention and have had great influence, even though some of them did not promote specifically theological themes. It is fair to say that these less academic writings initiated a comprehensive renewal of theology. Guardini's acceptance of an academic chair for "Philosophy of Religion and Catholic Weltanschauung" in Berlin in 1923 brought about a change in his life, above all in his scholarly pursuits and the unfolding of his singular kind of theology. It has been observed that "at the moment when Guardini said good-bye to academic theology, his theological thought began to take shape."[4] Subsequently, his numerous, diverse theological themes and perspectives emerged in his "many books." Although his spectrum of topics is broad, I will show the order of this vast literary corpus and note the intellectual orientation that met the special challenges of Guardini's day.

In the early 1920s, Guardini concerned himself above all with the meaning and form of the liturgy and the church. He gave a significant impulse not only to the liturgical movement but also to the ecclesial movement that led to the Second Vatican Council. He had an impact even upon the post-conciliar reform of the liturgy. One must name here his small, invaluable first book, *The Spirit of the Liturgy,* which appeared in 1918. No less important are the pedagogical and philosophical considerations in the book *Liturgische Buildung* (Liturgical Education) of 1923. However, towering above everything was Guardini's frequently quoted *The Church and the Catholic* of 1922, which treats the meaning and the shape of community within Catholicism.

Beginning in the 1930s, if not earlier, Guardini concentrated his theological reflection upon the figure and meaning of Jesus Christ. He saw not the church but the historical figure of Jesus as the proper "essence of Christianity," which he treated in the 1929 essay titled "The Essence of Christianity" and revised ten years later. In 1939, Guardini wrote his essay on "the image of Jesus the Christ in the New Testament" and the following year expanded it in his book *Jesus Christus: Sein Bild in den Schriften des Neuen Testaments* (Jesus Christ: His Image in the Writings of the New Testament).

During these same years, he provided spiritual access to the figure of Christ in a series of meditations that remain singular even today. These talks were assembled and edited in 1937 into the book *The Lord: Meditations upon the Person and Life of Jesus Christ.* Twenty years later, Guardini reflected on the "psychology" of Jesus in his book *The Humanity of Christ.* This work is Guardini's most distinctive contribution to christology, for it clearly moves away from conventional theological paths.

In many publications of the 1940s, Guardini treated the structure and content of the Christian faith and theology. In this effort, he was concerned about the "distinctiveness of Christianity," which is the title of a collection of his essays compiled in 1935. In particular, Guardini pressed the distinction between religion and revelation, between general religious experience and the specific material of a faith that is grounded in divine revelation. In 1940, he expressed his views in the short, though important work, *Offenbarung* (Revelation), and in 1958 he developed this theme further in his book *Religion und Offenbarung* (Religion and Revelation). (Unfortunately, both works are available only in German.) Related to this theme of revelation, Guardini undertook an "inquiry into the Christian teaching on human existence," which in 1939 appeared under the title *The World and the Person.* This same concern for theological anthropology led in 1944 to the book *Faith and Modern Man* and then in 1948 to *Freedom, Grace and Destiny.*

The 1950s are more clearly stamped than the preceding decades by Guardini's encounter with the spirit of the age. As early as 1927, in his *Letters from Lake Como,* Guardini described the issues and risks of a world dependent on modern technology. Then in 1950, he analyzed the contemporary state of affairs in a more programmatic manner in *The End of the Modern World.* Two years later he filled out his view of modern society in his penetrating study *Power and Responsibility.* In these writings, Guardini drew in particular on the recent, painful experience of Germany under Hitler and extended his insights to culture and politics at mid-century.

Along with the books that we have mentioned to this point, there are other, less explicitly theological works by Guardini that also deserve mention. These are the biographical studies and detailed interpretations of the writings of outstanding thinkers and poets. Beginning in the 1920s, Guardini worked a great deal on the literature of theologians and philosophers such as St. Augustine, Pascal and Kierkegaard and also on the writings of such literary figures as Dante, Dostoevski, Hölderlin and Rilke. These studies indirectly assisted Guardini's work on the "inner" life of Jesus. Their primary aim, however, was to show how that which is "distinctively Christian" comes to light in the literature and personalities of these great minds.

These biographical and literary studies reveal the intellectual orientation and unusual gifts of their author. Romano Guardini was not primarily interested in fashioning a systematic theology. In his teaching at the universities of Berlin, Tübingen and Munich, he desired above all to provide a comprehensive Catholic Christian Weltanschauung, or worldview. This intention did not lessen his theological orientation, since a Catholic Weltanschauung presupposes the Christian faith and remains closely associated with it.[5] In such a worldview, God does not remain an empty word or a mere fiction but is the all-encompassing reality which defines the world and human existence.

Romano Guardini was not primarily interested in fashioning a systematic theology. He desired above all to provide a comprehensive Catholic Christian worldview.

It is true, however, that this approach did not permit Guardini to speak directly about the primary datum of theology, namely, God. Instead his rigorous theological reflection was directed toward the world, because this is the concrete realm and context of human life. Given this orientation, Guardini provided clear perceptions of the world from the standpoint of faith and offered insights on living as a Christian in the modern age.

Because of this intellectual orientation, Guardini never belonged to a department of philosophy or a department of theology. He fit none of the usual classifications within the academy. Strictly speaking, he was neither a theologian nor a philosopher, neither a researcher nor a popularizer, neither an isolated thinker nor a religious commentator. Rather, he was all of these but nevertheless none of them purely and entirely. Current professional titles and categories describe neither him nor his writings, and they surely do not apply to the theology of this non-theologian. The inadequacy of our classifications shows itself above all when we consider the basic themes that recur in Guardini's writings.

The Theme That Determines Everything: Faith and Culture

When we inquire into Romano Guardini's primary interest, we immediately see that one theme predominates throughout his life: the theme of "faith and culture."[6] The expression "faith and culture" pinpoints two major topics, neither of which in itself receives a thorough analysis by Guardini. Guardini did not undertake specialized studies of each of these topics; rather, he focused on the interrelationship of faith and culture. He was convinced that Christian belief and culture are connected to each other and hence are more fruitfully understood in their mutual reciprocity. Drawing therefore on his

Christian faith, he developed his perceptions and intuitions regarding the modern world in which he lived.

One of the most striking features of Guardini's approach to the topic of faith and culture — a feature that subsequently influenced theology and the Second Vatican Council — was that he did not approach the contemporary world in a judgmental or patronizing manner. He was intent on attaining an unbiased view of "that which is." Therefore he sought to bring about an encounter that was neither rushed nor marked by arrogance so that the Christian faith and its theological reflection would emerge in dialogue with culture. It was with a remarkable openness, inquisitiveness and readiness to learn that Guardini made the effort to comprehend varied cultural forms. For him it was self-evident that theologians should study literary, political, social and technological expressions and seek to understand them in light of the Christian Weltanschauung. As early as 1915, he wrote that "a concrete expression of that which is meant by a 'Catholic worldview' appears in commentaries on culture."[7]

Here is situated the shift which Guardini brought about by means of his theology. Today, inspired by Vatican II, we regard Guardini's endeavor as an appropriate theological orientation, but this was not the case in the first half of the twentieth century. While today's theology sees that one of its tasks is to illumine the world in the light of Christian faith, in Guardini's time such an endeavor met resistance and required courage. At the time, it was seen by some to be an arrogant and elite undertaking in relation to matters that do not stand in immediate connection with Christian belief. At that time, faith and culture were seen as two separate and even opposing realities. In pursuing his kind of theology, Guardini led the way out of the theological ghetto and thereby produced a "new conception of theology. In this view, theology takes seriously the world as a genuine theological datum which is anchored in the inner life of God."[8]

For this reason, it is accurate to say that Guardini took decisive steps to bring about the stance toward the world that was adopted by the Second Vatican Council. In the *Pastoral Constitution on the Church in the Modern World* the Council expressly acknowledges the "autonomy of the earthly realities" as the legitimate realm of culture.[9] It stresses also that "the faithful ought to work in close connection with their contemporaries and try to get to know their ways of thinking and feeling, as they find them expressed in current culture."[10] This conciliar statement manifests the very conviction that determined Guardini's life and scholarship.

Furthermore, in proceeding as he did, Guardini appreciated that the phenomena of religious experience and religion have many forms of expression. For this reason, he paid careful attention to "the world of religious experience and religious acts . . . , to learning and culture, and to religious community and religious education."[11] He kept a watchful eye on "religious experience" and "religious personalities," for he was convinced that religion "involves the general human phenomenon of orientation to the divine, the study of which must be included in an analysis of culture."[12] Christian theology must take seriously this phenomenon of a universal, pre-Christian religious experience, because therein the "natural orientations of individuals and groups come to expression."[13] Moreover, these natural orientations retain their dignity and legitimate meaning in relation to the unfolding of Christian revelation.

At the same time, because culture contributes to the church's life and liturgy, the church protects and nurtures cultural forms, especially in times of cultural crises. In this vein, Guardini saw that the church is "the living reality that comes to maturity by means of the help of culture, which was given to it by Christ."[14] In other words, the Christian faith performs a vital service for culture when it adopts cultural forms for its worship, and conversely faith depends upon culture for its symbolic expression, objective forms and ordering of communal experience.

Guardini was aware, too, that the Christian faith must at times be critical of a specific culture in which it exists. Christian belief calls attention to the hazards of a culture and its non-Christian religious powers. Nevertheless, in exercising this role, Christian faith should not diminish the proper meaning of a culture and its various forms of expression. In fact, the positive role of Christian faith in relation to a culture remains foremost as the Christian Weltanschauung brings aspects of a culture into view. In this exchange, Guardini himself was led by his persistent concern "to bring into relationship the unconditional character of Christian faith with its view of reality and the world of culture."[15]

Guardini's new understanding of the relationship of faith and culture made a positive impact on the Second Vatican Council and can continue to have an impact today. It can guide us in our perceptions and assessment of the new religious interest that has awakened today outside the church.[16] We can hardly overlook the many and various ways in which today's culture is exhibiting forms of religious inquiry. We need to understand this phenomenon as an opportunity to bring the Christian faith into a fruitful exchange that may purify this deep, diffuse yearning for the transcendent that is making itself known.

In such an encounter the Christian faith cannot shirk its responsibility to play a critical role in relation to these new religious stirrings. Guardini himself spoke about faith's critique of contemporary religiosity in his 1923 book *Liturgische Bildung*. Reflecting on the religious awakening of the 1920s, he wrote,

We need to ask ourselves whether the religious vitality of our day is being clarified and expressed in our worship so as to realize the vision of "everything under Christ, our head." This religiosity is being manifest in our culture in a purely natural form, from natural feelings of piety rooted in a sense of our spiritual existence and existence in the world. It remains to be decided whether Christianity or paganism will determine the shape of this new religiosity, whether this new religious stirring will gain expression in the Catholic liturgy or in a heathen form of life as derived from the pagan piety of ancient Greece, Germany or the East. When viewed in this perspective, one of the most urgent challenges of our day concerns the role of the Christian liturgy in giving shape to today's spirit and our future.[17]

We can relate Guardini's comments to the present day and see alternatives not unlike the ones that Guardini perceived in his time. We face a situation similar to that of the 1920s, a critical juncture of Christian belief and culture at which we must decide whether to undertake a congenial but nonetheless critical reception of today's religious forces. Guardini's central theme of faith and culture remains, therefore, surprisingly current, even though we cannot adopt his answers but must find new ones for our time.

The Church as a Realm of Life and Jesus Christ as the Center of the Christian Faith

There is a second theme in Guardini's work that was ground-breaking for its day and still remains pertinent. In very difficult times, Guardini succeeded in recovering the Christian faith's living center, which had received little attention for many decades. At the turn of the century, the Catholic faith saw itself as a collection of many truths whose varying importance and deeper unity remained mostly hidden. At the same time, the Christian life was seen to be a matter of living according to predetermined ethical norms. In all of this, there was little sense, however, that to be Christian is to be a "disciple of Christ." Moreover, the church, with its liturgy and sacraments, was spoken of according to its formal aspects but not seen to be a community.

In this situation, which jeopardized the future of the Christian faith, Guardini understood the importance of overcoming the narrow and one-sided views that split up the consciousness of faith into many unconnected pieces. He promoted a view that showed the order of the whole of faith and linked all of its aspects to a center point. As a result, people could see more clearly how Christian faith is a genuine possibility of life. Guardini emphasized two elements of faith and thereby brought about a far-reaching shift in the church and theology, still long before Vatican II. Through his study of the liturgy, he discovered that the church is a realm of life constituted by the community of believers. With this insight, he pressed on and pinpointed the vital center of the church and its living tradition: Jesus Christ. These two aspects of Guardini's thought — his ecclesiology and christology — deserve brief comment.

Ecclesiology

Guardini saw that the liturgical movement of the early 1900s expressed a deeper stirring, namely, "an especially strong and remarkable movement for the 'renewal of the church.'"[18] He set out, therefore, to recover the sense of the church as a constitutive and living reality of faith. At the start of his book *The Church and the Catholic,* written in 1922, Guardini made his famous observation that a "religious process of unforeseen significance has occurred: the church is awakening in people's hearts."[19] He went on then to observe that the church is not something external to a believer's faith. It is not a rigid, juridical-institutional structure and thus not primarily an "official church." Rather, the church is above all the "body of Christ." It is the place where Christ still lives and acts in the world.

Guardini made concrete the idea of the body of Christ when he said that the community of believers represents the visible presence, the "body" of Christ in the world. With this insight, he contributed to the renewal of the Catholic consciousness of community. Although he did not explicitly employ the concept of the "people of God," Guardini conveyed this understanding when he stressed that the church is involved with the "incarnation" of human life and above all with "freedom." The church is not a barrier to interaction with the world but an opening to the world.

Moreover, Guardini described the church and the world as complementary realities. The church remains itself only when it reaches out to the world, when it sees itself as the "universal sacrament of salvation."[20] The church is, therefore, never its own goal. Also, it should not live a self-enclosed existence but must exist in and interact with the world. Only by means of this restless "existence in the world" will the church become ever more what it is and should become: the church of Jesus Christ. The church is the people of God, the body of Christ in the world, and as such the church manifests the coming into the world of Jesus Christ, the one who is the church's center and essence, its Lord.

The Second Vatican Council confirmed two basic elements of Guardini's ecclesiology, namely, that the church is a community and that the church is related to the world. Even today Guardini's theology of the church has significance. It challenges us to overcome one-sided, encrusted and confused views of the church so that we see the church as much more than structures and offices. The church is the realm of the Christian community within this world, the realm where the diversity of Christian existence is gathered to its ultimate center, where the community of faith shines forth with the result that this community is "the light of the world" and a "city built on a hilltop" (Matthew 5:14).

Christology

Guardini was not satisfied, however, to discuss the church alone. While recognizing the church as the community of Christian existence, he also knew that the church has a basis in history and a mission to which it is committed, even though this mission towers above the church. In his search for the "essence of Christianity," Guardini did not cling to the church itself nor did he look outside the church; rather, he delved into this community's foundation. Ahead of most other theologians, Guardini succeeded already in 1929 in presenting the "essence of Christianity" in a monograph with this title. Speaking of the church's center, he writes:

> There is no abstract definition of this essence. There is no doctrine, no basic structure of ethical values, no religious attitude and order of life which separates the person of Christ and the Christian reality. The Christian reality is Christ himself. . . . The Christian reality is therefore not a teaching of a truth or the meaning of life. To be sure, it includes this. But therein is not its essential kernel. Its essence is Jesus Christ himself, his concrete existence, his work and his destiny — this means therefore a historical person.[21]

In the 1970s, theologians including Walter Kasper and Hans Küng gave similar answers to the question concerning the essence of Christianity. But Guardini had already provided this answer 50 years earlier. Amid diverse understandings of the Christian faith, Guardini directed attention to the living center of Christianity, to the figure and message of Jesus. In numerous books, he attempted time and again to highlight the biblical figure of Jesus the Christ and to allow this person to be known as a living reality. At a time when the emphasis on Christ's divinity threatened a full understanding of his humanity, Guardini worked especially hard to recover the humanity of Jesus Christ.

In this effort, he deliberately refused to employ historical-critical methods in his interpretation of the Bible and instead relied on a "spiritual interpretation" of scripture. During Guardini's later years, theologians such as Hans Urs von Balthasar, Odo Casel, Yves Congar, Jean Daniélou, Henri de Lubac and Karl Rahner also committed themselves to the recovery of the essence of the Christian faith and in their search turned to the writings of the church Fathers. Guardini, however, went back to scripture and built his theology from this biblical foundation, not primarily from doctrinal formulations. To be sure, he acknowledged dogma, for he saw that it provides the direction for and the limits to new theological investigations. But at the same time, he regarded the doctrines themselves as too abstract and bloodless to express the living, personal reality of Christ and his concrete humanity. In view of the need for an existential faith, he saw dogma as at times a hindrance or, at best, a demand, a boundary stone and path marker, which we no longer would need when we have set our eyes and hearts upon Jesus Christ, the living Lord.

By means of this concentration on Jesus Christ, Guardini overcame the splintering of the consciousness of faith into many seemingly unconnected truths and recovered a new awareness of faith's center, Jesus Christ. This accomplishment remains one of Guardini's most valuable contributions to the church. It was realized above all in his book *The Lord* (1937), which for countless Christians opened the way to a vibrant faith in Christ. Moreover, by its reliance on the Bible, this book gave an impetus to the biblically grounded christology of our post-conciliar time.

Along with his emphasis on Jesus Christ, Guardini also discussed other elements of Christian belief. He concerned himself with the rosary and Mary. Moreover, he wrote about providence and grace. He also discussed the holy signs, such as the sign of the cross and holy water. Simultaneously, he exposed the challenging issues of modern culture. Nevertheless, Guardini never lost sight of faith's center point, Jesus Christ. In his judgment, this person provides the point of reference for the Christian Weltanschauung and therefore assures the fruitful dialogue between faith and culture. Guardini expressed this understanding in the 1920s when he wrote:

> Christ has the full view of the world. The perspective of Christ is the proper
> worldview. The believer enters into Christ. To believe means to enter into
> Christ, to attain the standpoint where Christ stands. . . . Therefore believers
> see the world clearly. They see it as it is. They see it in its entirety.[22]

As this statement makes evident, the church's center point, Jesus Christ, prompts Christians to undertake penetrating studies of the world and its culture.

Guardini's legacy and charge to our time is that we carry on the dialogue between Christian belief and culture. Those who are committed to the Christian faith cannot retreat from the world but must illumine the world's bright spots and shadows. They must not forget that their realm within the world remains the church as "the community of believers" and "the people of God." Moreover, they must see themselves as disciples of Jesus Christ, who is the basis for a new and true human existence in community, within the world and closely related to its many forms of culture.

Endnotes

This chapter was translated from the German text by Robert A. Krieg, CSC.

1. Without specifying every reference, this paper builds on the following interpretations of Guardini's work: Hans Urs von Balthasar, *Romano Guardini* (Munich: Kösel, 1970); Fridolin Wechsler, *Romano Guardini als Kerygmatiker* (Paderborn: Ferdinand Schöningh, 1973); Eugen Biser, *Interpretation und Veränderung: Werk und Wirkung Romano Guardinis* (Paderborn: Ferdinand Schöningh, 1979); Hans Mercker, *Christlicher Weltanschauung als Problem* (Paderborn: Ferdinand Schöningh, 1988); Alfons Knoll, *Glaube und Kultur bei Romano Guardini* (Paderborn: Ferdinand Schöningh, 1994).

   Some aspects of this chapter have been developed more fully in other writings by Arno Schilson: *Perspektiven theologischer Erneuerung* (Düsseldorf: Patmos, 1986); "Erneuerung der Sakramententheologie im 20. Jahrhundert," *Liturgisches Jahrbuch* 37 (1987): 17–41; "Romano Guardini und die Liturgische Bewegung," in Klemens Richter and A. Schilson (eds.), *Den Glauben feiern* (Mainz: Matthias Grünewald, 1989), 49–77; "Theologie als Mystagogie," in A. Schilson (ed.), *Gottes Weisheit in Mysterium* (Mainz: Matthias Grünewald, 1989), 203–30; "Romano Guardini und die Theologie der Gegenwart," *Theologie und Glaube* 80 (1990); 152–64; "Wiederbegegnung von Kult und Kultur," in Jürgen Hoeren (ed.), *Gott-Sucher im Spannungsfeld von Christentum und Moderne* (Würzburg: Echter, 1991), 41–58; "La sequela di Cristo, centro dell'esistenza cristiana. La Definizione dell'uomo secondo Romano Guardini," *Communio,* 132 (1993): 43–57. Essays on R. Guardini by various authors are found in A. Schilson (ed.), *Konservativ mit Blick nach vorn* (Würzburg: Echter, 1994).

2. See Romano Guardini, "Warum so viele Bücher?" in idem, *Stationen und Rückblicke* (Würzburg: Werkbund, 1965), 23–34. These "many books" are listed in Hans Mercker with the Katholische Akademie in Bayern (eds.), *Bibliographie Romano Guardini 1885–1968* (Paderborn: Ferdinand Schöningh, 1978).

3. See Alfons Knoll, "Die Seelen wiederfinden: Romano Guardini auf der Suche nach einer 'anderen' Theologie," in Schilson (ed.), *Konservativ mit Blick nach vorn,* 11–31.

4. Ibid., 23.

5. See Romano Guardini, "Vom Wesen katholischer Weltanschauung" (1923), in idem, *Unterscheidung des Christlichen. Gesammelte Studien 1923–1963* (Mainz: Matthias Grünewald, 1963), 12–33.

6. For a complete discussion of this theme, see Knoll, *Glaube und Kultur.*

7. Ibid., 62.

8. Mercker, *Weltanschauung,* 77; see also Knoll, *Glaube und Kultur,* 165.

9. See the Second Vatican Council, *Pastoral Constitution on the Church in the Modern World,* articles 36 and 53–62.

10. Ibid., 62.

11. Guardini's unpublished manuscript: "Der Zusammenhang des menschlichen Schaffens. Umriß einer Kulturphilosophie" (probably 1941), 72, cited in Knoll, *Glaube und Kultur,* 241.

12. Romano Guardini, *Religion und Offenbarung,* volume 1 (Würzburg: Werkbund, 1958), 11 and 15.

13. Ibid., 13.

14. See Guardini's early publication which he wrote under the pseudonym Anton Wächter, "Thule oder Hellas? Klassische oder deutsche Bildung?" in *Der Wächter* 3 (1920): 2 – 16, 66 – 79, here 77.

15. Romano Guardini, *Berichte über mein Leben,* ed. Franz Henrich (Düsseldorf: Patmos, 1984), 86.

16. See Schilson, *Gottes Weisheit.*

17. Romano Guardini, *Liturgische Bildung* (Burg Rothenfels am Main: Deutsches Quickbornhaus, 1923), 13.

18. Romano Guardini, *Vom Sinn der Kirche* (Mainz: Matthias Grünewald, 1955), 34.

19. Ibid., 19. On Guardini's ecclesiology, see Eva-Maria Faber, *Kirche zwischen Identität und Differenz. Die ekklesiologischen Entwürfe von Romano Guardini und Erich Przywara* (Würzburg: Echter, 1993).

20. This concept can be considered as a kind of key word for the ecclesiology of the Second Vatican Council. It appears in the *Dogmatic Constitution on the Church,* article 48.

21. Romano Guardini, *Das Wesen des Christentums* (Würzburg: Echter, 1938), 5, 68. This text first appeared in 1929.

22. Guardini, "Vom Wesen katholischer Weltanschauung," 24.

Chapter Four

North American Catholics' Reception of Romano Guardini's Writings

Robert A. Krieg, CSC

In his reflections on christology, the Dominican theologian Edward Schillebeeckx has made a point that applies not only to Jesus of Nazareth but to all human beings. According to Schillebeeckx, if we want to get to know someone, we need to look at more than the events and setting surrounding his or her life and at more than the people with whom he or she interacted. We must also consider the person's impact beyond his or her immediate world. In Schillebeeckx's words: "No individual can be understood . . . independently of the effect he has had on subsequent history or of what he might have intended to set in motion by direct action of his own."[1] This observation makes immediate sense with regard to the life of Jesus and also to the lives of all of us. In particular, it applies to our understanding of Romano Guardini.[2]

Even though Romano Guardini wrote his articles and books primarily for German Catholics, many of his texts in translation became guiding lights for English-speaking Catholics after the Second World War and through the Second Vatican Council.[3] This literature greatly improved the theological literacy of Catholic laity and clergy in Canada and the United States, and it prepared these Catholics for Vatican II's *aggiornamento*. Because of this deep influence of Guardini's thought on Catholicism in North America, it is important that this book include an appreciation of his impact on Catholics in the New World.

This study of the reception of Guardini's writings in North America consists of three parts. First, it reviews the publishing history of Guardini's books in English. Second, it considers the literature in English on Romano Guardini. And third, it highlights the comments on Guardini's writings by the Trappist monk Thomas Merton. To conclude, we discuss the reprinting of Guardini's books today.

Guardini's Writings in English

Romano Guardini's influence on the English-speaking world can be measured in part by statistics. This articulate, productive theologian wrote more than 70 books and 100 articles in German.[4] Of his writings, there have appeared in English at least 33 books, 10 excerpts from books, and 7 articles.[5] Five of these publications occurred from 1930 through 1935 and another five from 1948 through 1953. Eighteen texts by Guardini were translated into English from 1954 through 1959, and nineteen were published from 1960 through 1968. Beginning in 1954, two or three of his writings appeared every year in English. The peak year was 1957, when six texts by the then 72-year-old theologian were made available in English.

The exact figures concerning the distribution of books in English by Guardini are not available. One can guess that each book easily sold many thousands of copies. For instance, according to the publisher Henry Regnery, founder of the Henry Regnery Company, *The Lord* (in German, *Der Herr*) has sold well over 70,000 copies in Canada and the United States, and it remains in print.[6] (Worldwide, *Der Herr* has likely sold well over one million copies in its various translations.[7])

One thing shown by the statistics is that the reception of Guardini's writings among English speakers was delayed by the Second World War. Though his books and articles became well known in Germany beginning in 1918 with the publication of *Vom Geist der Liturgie,* they were virtually unknown in Canada and the United States until the mid-1950s. *Vom Geist der Liturgie* was translated into English in 1930 as *The Spirit of the Liturgy.* For the next 20 years, this marvelous text and nine others were all that was available in the English-speaking world, but they were not widely circulated in North America. Between 1935 and 1948, no texts by Guardini appeared in English. It was in 1954, with the publication of *The Lord,* that the name "Romano Guardini" became known to tens of thousands of North American Catholics. The immediate success of this one book helped create the market for the 36 other texts that appeared over the next 13 years. By the end of the 1960s, Catholics in Canada and the United States set aside Guardini's writings as they turned to theological writings inspired by the Second Vatican Council.

The difference in time between the publication of Guardini's writings in Germany and their publication in English extends, on occasion, to 30 years. *Vom Geist der Liturgie* appeared in 1918 but *The Spirit of the Liturgy* was published in 1930. This was Guardini's first book in English. *Vom Sinn der Kirche* (1922) was translated into English in 1935 under the title *The Church and the Catholic.* Though *Vom lebendigen Gott* came into print in 1929, it did not reach the English-speaking world until 1957 as *The Living God.* Guardini's *Die Bekehrung des Aurelius Augustinus* (1935) was not translated into *The Conversion of Augustine* until 1960. Similarly, his study of Blaise Pascal, *Christliches Bewußtsein* (1935) came out as *Pascal for Our Time* in 1966. *Der Herr* was published in 1937 and was introduced to readers of English in 1954 as *The Lord.*

In the case of Guardini's later writings, there was only a brief time between the German text and the English translation. *Das Ende der Neuzeit* was published in 1950, and *The End of the Modern World* appeared in 1956. The essay "Das Unendlich-Absolute und das Religiöse-Christliche" came into print in 1957 and the following year was published in English in the journal *Philosophy Today.* The meditations *Jesus Christus* were available in German in 1957, and in English, under the same title in 1959. Guardini's visionary statement of 1962 on the new Europe, titled "Europa," appeared in that same year in English. *Tugenden* was published in 1963 and was available four years later in English titled *The Virtues.* Guardini's last publication in English was *The Wisdom of the Psalms* in 1968, five years after its appearance in German.[8]

Along with the difference in time between a text's publication in German and its appearance in English, there is also the difference between the situation in Germany, where Romano Guardini wrote the original text, and the situation in North America, where the text was read in translation. As Guardini himself has acknowledged, he did not write his books according to an overall plan.[9] He was a situational writer whose texts were prompted by, and addressed to, the specific concerns and needs of his listeners and readers. These circumstances included Germany's "ghetto Catholicism" (that resulted from the *Kulturkampf*), the First World War, the liturgical movement, the rise of phenomenology, the youth movement, the emergence of biblical studies, the Weimar Republic, the tyranny of Adolf Hitler and National Socialism, the Second World War, the devastation of Germany and the "economic miracle" of the Federal Republic of Germany.[10]

These situations in Germany from the early 1900s through the 1960s bear little resemblance to the circumstances of Catholics in North America during these same decades. Though the two world wars made stiff demands on the people of Canada and the United States, these wars were not fought on the soil of the New World. In 1919, democracy was not a new form of government in North America as it was in Germany. The Great Depression was cruel to North Americans, but it did not impose the astronomical rates of inflation that were endured in the Weimar Republic, nor did it bring to Canada and the United States the bloody street fighting that took place in German cities between the Bolsheviks and the Free Corps.

Moreover, while Catholics in North America were immigrants and a minority within the predominantly Protestant society, they found opportunities for upward economic and social mobility throughout the twentieth century, as finally symbolized by the election of John F. Kennedy to the presidency of the United States in 1960.[11] By contrast, Catholics in Germany lived with relatively pronounced social stratification until after World War II. Thus, the social, economic and political experience of Guardini's North American readers possessed very few points of similarity to the situations in which Guardini gave birth to his books and articles.

The differences in time and circumstance made American publishers initially cautious about translating Guardini's books into English. A case in point is the decision of Henry Regnery to publish *The Lord*. Regnery, who in 1947 founded the Henry Regnery Company (now known as Regnery Gateway, Inc.), first learned of Romano Guardini when, after graduating from the Massachusetts Institute of Technology, he studied in Germany from 1933 to 1934. Afterward, in Chicago during the Second World War, he came to know Arnold Bergstrasser and Otto von Simson, both professors who had fled Germany and had been awarded academic appointments at the University of Chicago. It was Bergstrasser who introduced Regnery to Guardini's *Der Herr*.

In 1949, Regnery traveled to Germany, made contact with Guardini and his publisher Hans Waldmann, and received the publishing rights to *Der Herr* in English. Reluctant to pay the full cost of a professional translation, Regnery enlisted the services of Elinor Castendyk Briefs, who, with her husband, Goetz Briefs, a professor at Georgetown University, was a friend of Regnery. For a small stipend, Castendyk Briefs translated *Der Herr* into the clear, lyric English of the 535-page book *The Lord*. Much to the delight of Regnery and Castendyk Briefs, *The Lord* immediately became a best-seller. It was now evident that at least some of Guardini's books would sell very well in North America. Nevertheless, prior to having a text by Guardini translated into English for publication, Regnery would receive the assurance from the Thomas More Book Association that it would promote the book to the members of its book club.[12]

The importing of Guardini's texts into North America did not assure, however, that all dimensions of his writings would be appreciated by their English-speaking readers. Again, consider *The Lord*. In the 1930s, Guardini discussed Jesus Christ in comparison with Socrates and Buddha in his lectures at the University of Berlin, in his preaching to Berlin's Catholics at St. Benedict Chapel and in his spiritual conferences at Burg Rothenfels. (These lectures also resulted in the publication of Guardini's book *Der Tod des Socrates* in 1943.) He was intent upon emphasizing the absolute uniqueness of Jesus Christ. As a result, while Adolf Hitler presented himself as the Führer and the bearer of

God's grace, or *Heil,* Guardini was explaining that Jesus Christ alone is the Lord and the *Heil*-bringer, or savior.

In other words, *Der Herr,* appearing four years after Hitler's *Machtergreifung* (seizure of power) as Germany's chancellor, had an implicit criticism of National Socialism.[13] This point was not lost upon the Nazis, who sent spies to Guardini's lectures and liturgies with the aim of gathering evidence against the theologian so that, if need be, he could be arrested.[14] Unaware of the situation in which *Der Herr* was crafted, its North American readers of the 1950s and 1960s most likely did not catch the book's subtle denunciation of authoritarian rule in general and of Hitler's Reich in particular.

Unaware of the situation in which Der Herr was crafted, its North American readers most likely did not catch the book's subtle denunciation of authoritarian rule in general and of Hitler's Reich in particular.

These differences of time and situation did not, however, affect the reception of Guardini's writings among North American Catholics throughout the 1950s and 1960s. Though most Americans had little knowledge of Germany's liturgical movement, phenomenology movement and youth movement, they did not need such knowledge in order to value Guardini's writings, for Americans shared with Guardini the world-wide horizon of Catholic neoscholasticism, the Roman Rite for the eucharist and private devotions such as the Rosary and the Stations of the Cross. While they may have missed some dimensions of a text's implicit message (e.g., its criticism of Hitler), they obviously judged that they grasped Guardini's major ideas and knew how to apply them to circumstances in Canada and the United States.

Finally, we must call attention to the portrait of Guardini that English-speaking readers would have received from the selection of texts that were translated into English. When one glances through a list of Guardini's books in German, one immediately senses that their author is a Christian humanist and a "Renaissance scholar," an original thinker concerned with philosophy and the history of ideas, literature and psychology, culture and society, as well as with theology, liturgy and spirituality.

When one reviews the list of Guardini's books in English, however, one finds a more limited characterization of him. The majority of his writings available to North Americans treat liturgy and spirituality. These texts include *The Spirit of the Liturgy* (1930), *The Way of the Cross* (1932), *The Church and the Catholic* (1935), *Faith and Modern Man* (1952), *The Lord* (1954), *The Last Things* (1954), *Meditations Before Mass* (1955), *The Rosary* (1955), *Sacred Signs* (1956), *Prayer in Practice* (1957), *The Living God* (1957), *The Lord's Prayer* (1958), *Jesus Christus* (1959), *Prayers from Theology* (1959),

The Conversion of Augustine (1960), *Freedom, Grace, Destiny* (1961), *The Life of Faith* (1961), *The Word of God* (1963), *The Humanity of Christ* (1964), *Pascal for Our Time* (1966), *The Saints in Daily Christian Life* (1966), *The Church of the Lord* (1967), *The Virtues* (1967) and *The Wisdom of the Psalms* (1968).

To be sure, some of Guardini's other scholarly interests are represented by such books as *The Death of Socrates* (1948), *The End of the Modern World* (1956), *Power and Responsibility* (1961) and *Rilke's Duino Elegies* (1961). Texts of this sort have remained in the minority of the English translations, however, and most English-speaking Catholics have no idea that Guardini wrote thorough studies on Dante, Dostoevski and Hölderlin. As a result, they may have gained the impression that Guardini was primarily a spiritual writer, quite detached from cultural, scientific and social matters. If all they read were Guardini's books in English, they may lack even today an appreciation of the complexity and dialectical character of his thought.[15]

Articles in English on Guardini

To date there have appeared no books in English on the life and thought of Romano Guardini,[16] but English-speaking journals have discussed Guardini and his work for the past 60 years. The first article in English to treat Guardini was written by George Shuster in 1930, and since then Guardini has been the subject of at least 27 more articles.[17] Unfortunately, very few of these articles provide a detailed analysis of Guardini's key ideas, for example, concerning his understanding of divine revelation and his theory of opposites *(Gegensätze)*. Nevertheless, these essays have introduced Guardini's basic ideas and theological orientation. Moreover, most of Guardini's books in English have been reviewed in English-speaking journals. Since the early 1930s, at least 75 reviews have appeared. The books that have been most frequently reviewed are *The Death of Socrates* (1948), *The Lord* (1954) and *The End of the Modern World* (1956). Not surprisingly, the greatest number of articles and book reviews were written during the 1950s and 1960s.

One of the earliest essays in English on Guardini is A. N. Raybould's "In the Vanguard of Catholic Thought" (1933). Along with a discussion of Guardini's theology, it treats the thought of Jacques Maritain, Karl Adam, Dietrich von Hildebrand and Giovanni Papini. At the outset it observes that these five thinkers are "intimately connected with the Catholic movements of the moment: the Thomistic revival, the liturgical movement, youth groups, the ethical recall from pagan ideas."[18] Furthermore, because of these scholars' work, Catholicism "has gained in prestige with the non-Catholic public." Concerning Guardini in particular, the essay notes that he unites "depth of thought with perfection of expression." He is a master of language, whose writings hold up even in translation: "He himself knows how to create a language that is worthy of his thought." He is recognized as an influential leader in the liturgical movement and also as an outstanding professor at the University of Berlin. In these activities, Guardini "knows how to meet the young on their own ground, a master of intuitive psychology, he can understand them." Furthermore, he speaks and writes in a language that young people can readily grasp. "Guardini is not only a fascinating lecturer, he is one of the finest writers of modern Germany."[19]

Two articles are representative of the literature on Guardini that appeared in the 1950s and 1960s. Kurt Hoffman's "Portrait of Father Guardini" (1954) observes that Guardini had recently given a lecture in the series "Man in the Age of Technology," sponsored by the Bavarian Academy of Arts and Sciences, whose other speakers included the philosopher Martin Heidegger, the Nobel-prize physicist Werner Heisenberg, poet Friedrich Georg Juenger and artist Emil Preetorius. In this lecture, as in his other writings on modern society, Guardini had conjectured that "the modern age is drawing to an end. . . . We are standing on the threshold of a new age." That this theologian should be commenting on modernity is not surprising, Hoffman notes, when one realizes that throughout his life, Guardini brought new insights to many, diverse realms of thought. At the University of Berlin he had lectured on Dostoevski, Rilke and Hölderlin as well as on Augustine and Dante, and had drawn to his lecture hall not only students and professors but also Protestant and Catholic clergy and members of Berlin's high society. Away from Berlin at Burg Rothenfels, he gave retreat conferences and preached for young intellectuals, farmers and workers.[20]

Hoffman observes too that after World War II Guardini offered a new vision of Germany and Europe as he lectured at the University of Munich and served as an advisor to such influential people as Walter Dirks, the editor of the *Frankfurter Hefte,* and Clemens Münster, cultural director of Radio Munich — both of whom knew Guardini from their participation in the Quickborn. Along with Konrad Adenauer, he had urged after World War II that Germany assume the moral responsibility of paying reparations to Jews. Motivated by his understanding of the Christian faith, Guardini developed an extraordinarily wide breadth and depth of knowledge, and he spoke what he perceived to be the truth even when his comments made his listeners uncomfortable. Guardini "has provided discomfort for everyone who has thought he knew what Guardini was after and could sum it up in a simple sentence." Nevertheless, he had paradoxically become "one of the best loved and most influential persons in Germany today."

A second article on Guardini, "Faith Is the Center," appeared in *Time* magazine in 1960. Written on the occasion of the theologian's seventy-fifth birthday, it describes his modest apartment in Munich's suburb of Bogenhausen as "a center of Roman Catholic intellectual life in Germany." Here, with circles of students and scholars, Guardini conducted his "Laboratory of Ideas." Moreover, in his lecturing at the University of Munich and in his preaching at St. Ludwig Church, he spoke to "his thousands of German followers." In these diverse settings, he shared his insights on the psychology of Sigmund Freud and the painting of Paul Klee, the poetry of Friedrich Hölderlin and Rainer Maria Rilke, and the "Communist dialectic." In light of this wealth of knowledge, one of his students said that "Guardini is like a Renaissance humanist — he seems to have the key to everything."[21]

Time portrayed Guardini as "a center of Roman Catholic intellectualism" who lectured "eloquently on such disparate subjects as atomic science and Sigmund Freud, Paul Klee's paintings and the Communist dialectic."

The article also reviewed Guardini's career. After telling of his university studies and the immediate success of *Vom Geist der Liturgie* in 1918, it mentions that beginning in 1923 at the University of Berlin, Guardini "was one of the luminaries of an intellectually glittering city that included such disparate men as Producer Max Reinhardt, Conductor Wilhelm Furtwängler, Boxer Max Schmeling." Despite his fame in Berlin, he frequently immersed himself in the activities of the Quickborn at Burg Rothenfels, speaking with "workers, farmers and students, who eventually came from all over Germany." Dismissed from his professorship by the Nazi regime, he returned to the university lecture hall after the war, in Tübingen and Munich. In 1958, when the German government awarded him its prestigious honor *Pour le mérite,* the Protestant newspaper *Basler Nationalzeitung* wrote that Guardini was "one of the great religious figures of our time." *Time* concluded by observing that "Guardini has founded no theological schools, and his power lies more in the eloquence of his preaching and writing than in any specific theories."

On the occasion of Guardini's death on October 1, 1968, obituaries appeared in English. *Time* portrayed Guardini as "a center of Roman Catholic intellectualism" who lectured "eloquently on such disparate subjects as atomic science and Sigmund Freud, Paul Klee's paintings and the Communist dialectic." It again characterized Guardini as "a Renaissance humanist."[22] *The New York Times* described Guardini as a "Roman Catholic religious philosopher" and then summarized the article that appeared in *Time* in 1960.[23] London's *Tablet* spoke of Guardini as "one of the most influential and popular theologians and philosophical writers of the twentieth century," whose most important contribution was "his gift for applying his own strikingly original conception of philosophical and theological ideas to social, political and aesthetic problems." Recipient of the Erasmus Prize in 1962, he insisted that "Catholic intellectuals . . . take full account of the values of their contemporaries, and of the social and intellectual challenges of their time."[24] In concluding, it noted that Archbishop Julius Cardinal Döpfner of Munich presided at the Requiem Mass and that messages of "tribute and condolence" had been received from Pope Paul VI and President Heinrich Lübke of Germany.

Since his death, at least nine articles have appeared in English about Romano Guardini. Representative of these is the entry by Paul Misner in the *New Catholic Encyclopedia*'s supplementary volume of 1974. After a review of Guardini's career and the significance of *Vom Geist der Liturgie* (1918) and *Vom Sinn der Kirche* (1922), Misner says of Guardini: "In German-speaking lands there is no one who deserves more to be called a precursor of Vatican Council II." An overview of Guardini's literary corpus concludes with the observation that the underpinning for these diverse writings is the theologian's dialectical outlook. In Misner's words:

> The common background of the immense variety of subjects he treated was his philosophical theory of polar opposition (*Der Gegensatz,* 1925). This proved to be an extraordinarily fruitful starting point from which to bring revelation (*Religion und Offenbarung,* 1950) and world reality (*Welt und Person,* 1939; *The End of the Modern World,* 1950; *Power and Responsibility,* 1951) into a synthesis.[25]

Statements similar to this one by Misner have helped Guardini's English-speaking readers pay attention to the complexity of his thought. The impression of Guardini given by the selection of his books that were translated into English has therefore been enriched and extended by the articles in English about Guardini. These 28 or more articles have served the theologian well, for they have presented him as a "Renaissance humanist."

Thomas Merton

One other source to which we can turn in order to appreciate the reception of Romano Guardini's writings in the English-speaking world is the cluster of influential Catholics who read Guardini's works and afterward strongly recommended them to others. This group includes the writer Flannery O'Connor (1925 – 1964), the social activist Dorothy

Day (1897–1980), who founded the Catholic Worker movement, and the Trappist monk Thomas Merton.[26] Here, we will consider only the comments on Guardini's works by Thomas Merton.

Thomas Merton was born on January 31, 1915, in Prades, France, and died on December 10, 1968, in Bangkok, Thailand. He ranks among the most outstanding American Catholic writers of the twentieth century.[27] After studying at the University of Cambridge and earning academic degrees at Columbia University in New York City (1938 and 1939), he taught English at Columbia University and at St. Bonaventure University in Olean, New York. Having been received into the Catholic Church in 1938, he entered the Trappist Abbey of Gethsemani, near Louisville, Kentucky, in December 1941. He was ordained a priest in 1949.

As a Trappist monk, Merton initially wrote numerous poems, which were published in collections such as *Figures for an Apocalypse* (1948). He received international fame after the publication of his autobiography, *The Seven Storey Mountain* (1948), in which he recounts how his journey of faith led him to a life of contemplation. Throughout the late 1940s and into the 1960s, Merton produced inspiring, insightful spiritual writings such as *Seeds of Contemplation* (1949), *The Sign of Jonas* (1953) and *The Living Bread* (1956). Beginning in the early 1960s, as the United States underwent the turmoil of the Civil Rights movement, the Vietnam War and student demonstrations, Merton extended his penetrating gaze to social and political matters in *Conjectures of a Guilty Bystander* (1966) and *Contemplation in a World of Action* (1971), among other writings. Simultaneously, he studied the monasticism and contemplative life of non-Christian religions. Sadly, while attending an international monastic convention in Bangkok, he was electrocuted by a faulty wire on his window fan. One expression of his inquiry into world religions is *The Asian Journal of Thomas Merton* (1973).

Merton's observations on the writings of Romano Guardini are made all the more interesting by the fact that Guardini himself read the writings of the Trappist monk and on at least two occasions commented on them. In November 1954, Guardini wrote in his journal:

> I am very moved by the book by Thomas Merton: *The Sign of Jonas* [1953]. Previously I had considered the influence of the American spirit in religious matters to be simply negative. This was incorrect. Merton can also bring it about that things receive a singular immediacy; they become simple and fresh.[28]

Guardini expanded on this comment four years later. In an interview he said that his reading of Merton's writings had given him the impression that Merton should refrain from writing for a period of time so that he could give birth to a book of exceptional quality. Referring to Merton, Guardini observed:

> Some of his books are very good indeed. But sometimes I think if he would find a way to withdraw from this activity for a few years, maybe he would then produce a truly great book for our age.[29]

With this knowledge of Guardini's words on the writings of Thomas Merton, we can turn to Merton's views on Guardini's works.

Like most Americans, Merton seems to have begun to read Guardini's writings in the 1950s. The first known reference to Guardini occurred in a journal entry of August 31, 1958. Guardini's *Das Gebet des Herrn* (1932) appeared in English in early 1958 under the title *The Lord's Prayer*. In the previous year, Guardini's *Vorschule des Betens* (1943) had been translated into English as *Prayer in Practice*. Both works by Guardini include extensive discussions on divine providence. Apparently in reference to *The Lord's Prayer*, Merton wrote in his journal:

> Always very fine ideas in Guardini on Providence. For instance that the will of God is not a "fate" to which we submit but a creative act in our life producing something absolutely new (or fail to do so), something hitherto unforeseen by the laws and established patterns. Our cooperation (seeking first the Kingdom of God) consists not solely in conforming to laws but in opening our wills out to this creative act which must be retrieved in and by us — by the will of God.
>
> This is my big aim — to put everything else aside. I do not want to create merely for and by myself a new life and a new world, but I want God to create them in and through me. This is central and fundamental — with this one can never be a mere Marxian communist.[30]

One of Guardini's books to which Merton frequently referred was *Pascal for Our Time* (1966). In a letter dated January 20, 1967, to the Argentine poet Victoria Ocampo, Merton wrote: "I have just read a beautiful book by Guardini on Pascal: this same Pascal who so fascinated and repulsed Camus."[31] A couple of months later he wrote the following in a "circular letter" to his friends:

> I have in fact just been reading Romano Guardini's excellent little book on Pascal [*Pascal for Our Time*]. He analyzes the "demon of combativeness" in Pascal — a demon which is no prerogative of Jansenists. At times one wonders if a certain combativeness is not endemic in Catholicism: a "compulsion to be

always right" and to prove the adversary wrong. A compulsion which easily leads to witch-hunting and which, when turned the wrong way, hunts its witches in the church herself and finally needs to find them in Rome. There are always human failures which can be exploited for this purpose. Pascal nearly went over the falls completely, but he recognized the destructiveness of his own inner demon in time, and knew enough to be silent and to believe. And to love. The story of his death is very moving.[32]

Merton's delight in *Pascal for Our Time* has been described by his close friend John Howard Griffin, who writes concerning Merton in early January 1967:

> With the return of cold weather, the hermit turned to Guardini's study of Pascal . . . whom he described as "my kind." The book so stimulated him that he had to stop frequently and walk around the hermitage in order to absorb the rush of ideas. "Yes, I know," he wrote, "the world is full of people who will want me to know that my reading of Pascal is vicious — like taking LSD. Fatal pessimism and all that. Jansenism."[33]

Turning to the Trappist monk's letters, we note that he frequently recommends Guardini's writings. To Czeslaw Milosz on February 28, 1959, he writes: "Among the Catholics, Bouyer is writing some good things, also of course De Lubac, Daniélou, etc. And then there is Guardini, who is splendid."[34] In July 1962, Merton recommended to a new director of novices that *Prayer in Practice* is an "excellent" book, especially for men and women entering religious life.[35] In a letter to Mario Falsina on March 25, 1967, Merton discussed the "European and American thinkers who have influenced me." For the "modern theological writers" he lists "Hans Urs von Balthasar, De Lubac, Daniélou, Bouyer, Dom Leclerq, K. Rahner, Romano Guardini, Jacques Maritain, E. Gilson."[36]

Finally, in *Conjectures of a Guilty Bystander* (1966), Merton turns to the writings of Guardini as he reflects on the social change underway in the United States. Although he does not cite a text by Guardini, he seems to be recalling ideas that are expressed in *The End of the Modern World* (1956) and *Power and Responsibility* (1961). For instance, Merton refers to the thought of Romano Guardini when he considers that because Christians stand somewhat outside the mainstream of modern society, they are in a position to enter into the world and assist it to become more than it currently is. In Merton's view, Guardini sees "the solitude of a Christian in a world detached from Christian order" and judges that Christians cannot remain satisfied standing on the sidelines and saying that the world is in error. They are beckoned by God to enter into the world to bring about God's intention for the world. Merton states: "Guardini is speaking of the true situation of the Christian in the world today: called by what does not yet exist, called to help it come into existence *through and by a present dislocation of Christian life.*"[37]

In summary, Thomas Merton greatly valued the writings of Romano Guardini. In Gethsemani Monastery, situated among the gentle hills of western Kentucky, this Trappist monk was separated from the German theologian by both time and circumstance. Nevertheless, he marveled at the unusual wisdom contained in Guardini's texts. In voicing his high regard for Guardini's writings, Merton spoke for tens of thousands of Catholics in North America.

Whether to Reprint Guardini's Texts Today

Some North Americans are currently urging publishers to print new editions in English of Romano Guardini's writings. They argue that since most of the English texts by Guardini are out of print, many Catholics in North America can no longer benefit from this theologian's insights. On occasion they also note that in Germany new editions of Guardini's writings are currently appearing.[38] As a result of this renewed interest in Guardini's writings, Sophia Institute Press has recently reprinted *Meditations Before Mass* (original German 1939), *Prayer in Practice* (original German 1943) under the new title of *The Art of Praying* and *The Rosary* (original German 1940). William B. Eerdmans has provided an English translation of *Letters from Lake Como*. It is appropriate, therefore, to consider the value and the risk of reprinting Guardini's texts at this time.

The value of publishing anew Guardini's books in English is that his writings, drawing on the humanist heritage of the West and also on the teachings of the church, offer a limpid synthesis of Christian humanism prior to the Second Vatican Council. There are few books today that offer Guardini's encompassing view of our existence before God. Moreover, some of Guardini's books may qualify as classics. That is, they possess a wisdom that transcends the context in which the writings appeared.[39] In this regard, one immediately thinks of *The Spirit of the Liturgy, The Virtues* and *The Wisdom of the Psalms*.

Nevertheless, there is also a risk involved in publishing Guardini's works anew today in North America. It may happen that these books will be understood by their readers to convey an intention that goes contrary to Guardini's original intention. To be concrete, some of Guardini's texts can be misconstrued now to support a neoconservative or "restorationist" agenda. They can seem to convey the message that today's Christians should withdraw from secular society and form an alternative community, not unlike a sect. Such an understanding, of course, goes contrary to Guardini's persistent efforts to overcome "ghetto Catholicism" and nurture a "cultural Catholicism," a Catholicism in dialogue with its age.

Indeed, Guardini himself maintained a rich exchange between the Judeo-Christian scripture and tradition on the one hand and modern thought on the other. He was convinced of the necessity of having the church's teachings challenge contemporary thought and values and, conversely, of having contemporary thought and values ask hard questions of Christian belief. This conviction rests on Guardini's insight that "a fruitful illumination of Christian existence is attained through this process of an ever new and changing encounter [between Christian faith and the world]."[40] Hence, it would violate Guardini's lifelong intention if his writings were misinterpreted to call for a fortress mentality against modernity.

Guardini was convinced of the necessity of having the church's teachings challenge contemporary thought and values and, conversely, of having contemporary thought and values ask hard questions of Christian belief.

Why might the underlying intention of Romano Guardini's texts be misconstrued today among English speakers? First, the Second Vatican Council has brought about a major shift in the horizon of religious meaning among Roman Catholics. Today's North American readers lack a knowledge of the economic, political and social world in which Guardini wrote his original texts. They share this ignorance with North American readers of the 1950s and 1960s, but unlike the earlier generation, they also differ from Guardini in their experience of worship, church life and theology. The pre–Vatican II Catholic "world" no longer exists. Today it is either forgotten or unknown. To read Guardini's texts out of this context of meaning may result in their misinterpretation.

Second, since the Second Vatican Council, the theological disciplines have undergone significant changes in their methods and central issues. For instance, scriptural study now relies on a host of historical and literary methods, and christology depends upon approaches "from below" as well as "from above." Furthermore, ecclesiology is addressing such issues as collegiality among bishops and lay ministry, and liturgical study is inquiring into issues of culture, ritual and symbol. Because Guardini does not employ these new methods or speak to these pressing current issues, he could be wrongly perceived as opposing them. In fact, Guardini must be remembered for his intellectual courage, open-minded inquiry and readiness to enter into dialogue with contemporary ideas.

How then should English-speaking publishers proceed with Guardini's works? First, they should be judicious in their selection of texts. They must favor the books that are the classics and avoid the works that manifest pre–Vatican II methods and issues. Second, they should provide each book with an introduction. This introduction should describe the situation to which the text was originally addressed, highlight the text's major theological themes and explain how this text helped prepare the way toward Vatican II. In some cases, the introduction should also call attention to the ways in which Guardini's methods or ideas have been surpassed in post–Vatican II theology. In short, these introductions could imitate the introductions that are now included in the new German editions of Guardini's books, though they would need to be more extensive than their German counterparts.

In our review of the reception of Guardini's writings among English-speaking Catholics, we have seen that these texts were highly valued by Catholics in Canada and the United States during the 1950s and 1960s. They were taken to heart by these Catholics because they were seen to convey an exceptional wisdom, a wisdom in which could be heard the word of God. In his book *The Wisdom of the Psalms,* Guardini makes a comment about wisdom that Catholics in North America throughout the 1950s and 1960s would have applied to Guardini's own writings: "Wisdom is something different from knowledge. . . . Wisdom means the ability to distinguish between what leads to life and what leads, however distantly, to death."[41]

In the judgment of thousands of Catholics in Canada and the United States, the writings of Romano Guardini led to life — life for individual readers and life also for the entire church which, thanks in part to Guardini's work, was to some extent ready for the *aggiornamento* of the Second Vatican Council. If we are to remain true to Guardini's wisdom, then we must go beneath the letter of his texts and discover their spirit of renewal and hope.

Endnotes

1. Edward Schillebeeckx, *Jesus,* trans. by Hubert Hoskins (New York: Crossroad, 1979), 44.

2. There exists a wealth of literature in German on the life and thought of Romano Guardini. These writings include Eugen Biser, *Interpretation und Veränderung* (Paderborn: Ferdinand Schöningh, 1979); Hanna-Barbara Gerl, *Romano Guardini* (Mainz: Matthias-Grünewald, 1985); Arno Schilson, *Perspektiven theologischer Erneuerung* (Düsseldorf: Patmos, 1986); Hans Mercker, *Christliche Weltanschauung als Problem* (Paderborn: Ferdinand Schöningh, 1988); Alfons Knoll, *Glaube und Kultur bei Romano Guardini* (Paderborn: Ferdinand Schöningh, 1993).

3. This chapter is a revised version of an essay that appeared in Wilhelm Geerlings and Max Scheler (eds.), *Kirche sein,* In Honor of Hermann Josef Pottmeyer (Freiburg im Breisgau: Herder, 1994), 93–100. It is printed here with the permission of Herder Verlag.

4. An invaluable resource is Hans Mercker with the Katholische Akademie in Bayern (eds.), *Bibliographie Romano Guardinis, 1885–1968* (Paderborn: Ferdinand Schöningh, 1978).

5. Many of the articles in English by Guardini appeared in *Cross Currents* and *Philosophy Today.* Excerpts from his books were frequently published in *Jubilee* and *Catholic Digest.*

6 This information was learned during a personal interview with the publisher Henry Regnery in Chicago, Illinois, on August 3, 1993.

7. "Faith Is the Center," *Time* 75 (March 14, 1960): 51.

8. For a fuller list of Guardini's books in English and the date of their publication in German, see the selected bibliography at the end of this book.

9. Romano Guardini, "Warum so viele Büchern?" (1955), in idem, *Stationen und Rückblicke* (Würzburg: Werkbund, 1965), 30.

10. On the recent history of the Catholic Church in Germany, see Gordon A. Craig, *Germany 1866–1945* (New York: Oxford University Press, 1978); Hubert Jedin and John Dolan (eds.), *History of the Church,* vol. 9: *The Church in the Industrial Age,* trans. Margit Resch (New York: Crossroad, 1981); Hubert Jedin, Konrad Repgen and John Dolan (eds.), *History of the Church,* vol. 10: *The Church in the Modern Age,* trans. Anselm Biggs (New York: Crossroad, 1981).

11. On the history of Catholics in the United States, see Jay Dolan, *The American Catholic Experience* (Garden City: Doubleday, 1985).

12. I am indebted to the publisher Henry Regnery for this information.

13. Guardini gave this criticism in his essay "Der Heiland," *Die Schildgenossen* 14 (1935) and subsequently made it even more explicit in his book *Der Heilbringer in Mythos, Offenbarung und Politik* (Stuttgart: Deutsche Verlagsanstalt, 1946).

14. Gerl, *Romano Guardini,* 246–47; Heinz Hürten, *Deutschen Katholiken 1918–1945* (Paderborn: Ferdinand Schöningh, 1992), 455. Also, for this information, I am indebted to Heinz R. Kuehn and Regina Kuehn of Oak Park, Illinois.

15. This limited characterization is unfortunate. It leaves Guardini vulnerable to being misrepresented as standing within a conservative orientation. Such a one-sided view of Guardini is conveyed in Massimo Borghesi, "Reflection: A New Beginning," *30 Days* 5 (1992): 62–68.

16. A book in English on Guardini's theology is currently being written by R. Krieg. Also, Hans Urs von Balthasar's *Romano Guardini* (1970) has been translated into English by Albert K. Wimmer and will soon be published by Ignatius Press.

17. George N. Shuster, "The Several Humanists," *The Commonweal* 11 (April 2, 1930): 613–15.

18. A. N. Raybould, "In the Vanguard of Catholic Thought," *Catholic World* 137 (1933): 658–66, 658.

19. Ibid., 661.

20. Kurt Hoffman, "Portrait of Father Guardini," *The Commonweal* 60 (September 17, 1954): 575–77.

21. "Faith Is the Center," *Time,* 51.

22. "Milestones," *Time* 92 (October 11, 1968): 102.

23. "Romano Guardini, Theologian, Dead," *The New York Times* (October 2, 1968): 39.

24. "Death of Romano Guardini," *Tablet* 222 (October 12, 1968): 1021.

25. Paul Misner, "Guardini, Romano," in David Eggenberger (ed.), *New Catholic Encyclopedia,* vol. 16: *Supplement 1967–1974* (Washington, D.C.: Publishers Guild, Inc., with McGraw-Hill Book Company, 1974), 198–99.

26. On Dorothy Day's reading of Guardini, see William D. Miller, *Dorothy Day: A Biography* (San Francisco: Harper and Row, 1982), 198, 234, 413. On Flannery O'Connor's reading of Guardini, see Rose Bowen, "Christology in the Works of Flannery O'Connor," *Horizons* 14 (1987): 7-23.

27. Studies of the life and thought of Thomas Merton include Michael Mott, *The Seven Mountains of Thomas Merton* (Boston: Houghton Mifflin Company, 1984); Anne E. Carr, *A Search for Wisdom and Spirit* (Notre Dame: University of Notre Dame Press, 1988); Lawrence S. Cunningham (ed.), *Thomas Merton: Spiritual Master* (New York: Paulist Press, 1992).

28. Romano Guardini, *Wahrheit des Denkens und Wahrheit des Tuns* (Paderborn: Ferdinand Schöningh, 1980), 98. Editor's note: Unless otherwise noted, this chapter's translations from the German are by R. Krieg.

29. Joseph B. Gremillion, "Interview with Romano Guardini," *America* 100 (November 15, 1958): 194–95.

30. Merton's journals are currently being edited by Lawrence S. Cunningham, who kindly made this entry available.

31. Thomas Merton, *The Courage for Truth: The Letters of Thomas Merton to Writers,* edited by Christine M. Bochen (New York: Farrar, Straus and Giroux, 1993), 210.

32. Thomas Merton, *The Road to Joy: The Letters of Thomas Merton,* selected and edited by Robert E. Daggy (New York: Farrar, Straus and Giroux, 1989), 97.

33. John Howard Griffin, *Follow the Ecstasy, The Hermitage Years 1965–1968* (Fort Worth, Texas: JHG Editions, 1983), 135–36.

34. Merton, *The Courage for Truth,* 56.

35. Thomas Merton, *The School of Charity: The Letters of Thomas Merton,* selected and edited by Brother Patrick Hart (New York: Farrar, Straus and Giroux, 1990), 145.

36. Merton, *The Road to Joy,* 349.

37. Thomas Merton, *Conjectures of a Guilty Bystander* (New York: Doubleday, 1966), 284–85.

38. The new editions of Guardini's books in German are being promoted by the Katholische Akademie in Bayern and Matthias-Grünewald Verlag.

39. On the nature of a classic, see David Tracy, *The Analogical Imagination* (New York: Crossroad, 1981), 99–115.

40. Romano Guardini, "Wahrheit und Ironie" (1965), in idem, *Stationen und Rückblicke,* 43.

41. Romano Guardini, *The Wisdom of the Psalms,* trans. Stella Lange (Chicago: Henry Regnery, 1968), 131.

Chapter Five

Romano Guardini as Sapiential Theologian

Lawrence S. Cunningham

Some years ago I was asked by a prominent editor of an American publishing house about what needed "to be done" in Catholic publishing. My reply was that books which had received a certain level of acceptance written before the Second Vatican Council should be put back into print. Which ones, the editor queried? Thinking of my own pleasure at having encountered *The Spirit of the Liturgy* and *The Lord,* I replied: Begin with Romano Guardini.

That, in fact, has not happened in the United States except for a few titles published in rather out-of-the-way places. The almost total erasure of Guardini's legacy in the English-speaking world has always struck me as an anomaly. Is it the case that he is a "period person" whose life and work now represent only evidence for what has been? Are those who wish to read him today simply *laudatores temporis acti?* Does he belong with Odo Casel, Ildefons Herwegen, Josef Pieper, Hugo Rahner and company as merely a name prominent in a German Catholic moment now surpassed by the events of the Council and post-conciliar history?

In a sense, those writers certainly are. One piece of evidence is that when, in preparation for this paper, I decided to get some Guardini volumes for my own library, I had to turn to the specialized theological booksellers of used books. It was a consolation, though, to learn that as fast as they could find the volumes they would sell them to a small but appreciative audience. Guardini, at least in this country, is for many now a name for the antiquarian book dealers and their select public.

There is a further point: When asked to participate in this conference, it occurred to me, on reflection, that I had not read Guardini for nearly 25 years. What I remembered about him was the pleasure I had in reading those books which came from Regnery and Pantheon so regularly when I was in my university studies. This paper, in fact, reflects a selective rereading rather than a sustained conversation with his thought. What I have read, finally, I read with an eye to underlying themes and not to "correct" Guardini's theology from the perspective of such advances as may have occurred over the past generation or so.

Locating Guardini

Romano Guardini died in October 1968. Two months later the Trappist author Thomas Merton was accidentally electrocuted in Thailand. Their lives were strikingly different but their Weltanschauung (worldview) was not. Both were deeply indebted to monastic spirituality (Guardini was a lifelong oblate of the Benedictines); neither wrote within the context of scholastic theology; both were strongly rooted in the sapiential understanding of the scriptures; both were committed to reflecting on the belletristic culture of our time; both were prodigiously productive as writers; and both — though from far different social locations — were at home with the main currents of contemporary culture. Finally, both men's writings were difficult to classify; they were not spiritual writers in the way that, say, a Dom Columba Marmion was a spiritual writer, nor were they theologians in the way a Karl Rahner was a theologian. They both stood in the interstices of modern Catholic thought and, in their lifetimes, were prodigiously influential. Merton, however, is still widely read in this country and Guardini is not.

I am neither a prophet nor the child of a prophet, so I do not know if there will be a Guardinian renaissance in the English-speaking world. Nor am I fully convinced that there ought to be one. I do have a conviction, however, that could serve as the thesis of this paper and it is this: that the *kind* of theology Guardini did should always find a place in the church. If he cannot be resurrected *qua persona,* his life and work does point, nonetheless, to the kind of intellectual life that the church should nourish. In that sense, at least, the professional life of Guardini offers suggestions about urgent contemporary theological tasks. He might serve as a template or paradigm for one kind of theology that today is somewhat neglected.

Note that I call Romano Guardini (as well as Thomas Merton) a theologian. I do so because there is an older understanding of the theologian as one who speaks compellingly of God; I do not claim that either is a theologian in the more recent academic sense in which the word is used. My basic thesis is this: Romano Guardini teaches us what it means to be a *sapiential theologian, sapiential* because he was a seeker of wisdom and *theologian* in the sense of the old patristic meaning of theologian: one who speaks experientially of God.[1]

Guardini as Theologian

It is, in the first instance, easier to say what kind of theologian Guardini was not. In a recent introductory essay to a Karl Rahner anthology, Karl Lehmann notes that Rahner set his career in the midst of the academic theology of his time with the simple strategy of remolding neo-scholastic theology with an appeal to history. Lehmann then adds:

> To be sure, there were always important theologians — such as Romano Guardini and Hans Urs von Balthasar — who simply set up shop *alongside* the marketable scholastic theology. But their thinking was, more often than not, unrelated to it. These undoubtedly influential thinkers, therefore, did not have a transformative effect precisely where dogmatic theology was translated into the church's lived life, in the day-in and day-out theology of the schools.[2]

Guardini at the
age of 70, in 1955.

That strikes me as essentially correct. Von Balthasar, to cite a case, is influential in certain circles today, but he was largely marginalized at the time of the council. In my own formal theological training, done on the cusp of the council, I did not hear the name of Guardini mentioned (he was a "spiritual writer" and, hence, in the province of the spiritual director) even though I read him all through the late 1950s and early 1960s. Furthermore, and perhaps for quite complex reasons, neither Guardini nor von Balthasar were invited to serve as *periti* at the Council.

Guardini's work was aimed at an audience that was not at home in the confines of the theology classroom; his work was for an *ad hoc* audience composed of the university population and the educated public. It was not oriented to the seminary *aula* and hence, due to this lack of inward turn, did not engage what would become the great issues of the council even though Guardini's life was, as it were, a prophetic voice (e.g., with regard to the liturgy) that anticipated the council. In a very real sense, Guardini chose a path that did not afford him a position of power in the theological revolution that was to take place in the postwar period. Guardini's work also was a theology that was apologetic but without the rationalist clang of syllogisms that characterized much of apologetics earlier in this century.

Guardini did some of his most fruitful work in the aftermath of, and in the context of, Rome's condemnation of Modernism. More than one commentator on Guardini insists that the arena within which he worked was at least in part a hedge against the inquiries of the Integralists, the ultraconservatives during the pontificate of

Pius X. He stayed away from critical studies on the scriptures; he did not engage any sustained critique of the regnant manual Thomism of the day (his choice of Bonaventure for his early research was a happy stroke both for his field of inquiry and for the future shape of his outlook); and, finally, his chair was not in theology narrowly understood. It is worthwhile recalling that when Karl Rahner assumed Guardini's chair at Munich in 1963, he did not have the right to direct dissertations in theology.[3]

Guardini's Theological Perspective

Romano Guardini was a person of adamantine faith. His Catholic worldview rested on two pivotal points: a total acceptance of the doctrine of creation and his equal conviction that God revealed himself to us through the Word. Indeed, those twin convictions made it possible, in his own mind, for philosophy to intersect with the theology that had so enlightened one of his early auditors in Berlin, Hans Urs von Balthasar. Is it too wide of the mark to insist that one of the most important offsprings of Guardini's work is to be seen in the magisterial work produced by von Balthasar in the early 1960s?[4]

If one combines these foundational beliefs in creation and revelation with Guardini's hermeneutical principle of *der Gegensätze* (opposites), one sees with what facility Guardini was able to mount simultaneously a defense against post-Enlightenment pretensions and an apologia for the Christian faith. For if it is true that God reveals both through the universe as given and through concrete historical events (notice how these affirmations restate the two books of medieval theology: *liber naturae/liber scripturae*), then one has an axial point with which both to critique and to affirm when engaged with the larger (secular) culture. The principle of *der Gegensätze,* in short, allowed Guardini to live in the post-Enlightenment world while simultaneously making appeal to a transcendental criterion (revelation) so that the acids of modernity could be neutralized.

These twin foundational points were assumed in faith by Guardini; he did not spend his time justifying them. His interest was in spelling out the implications of what a world (*our* world) and history looks like when these two facts are taken as a starting point.

A persistent theme in Guardini's writings, rooted in these twin doctrines of creation and revelation, was the conviction that to lose sight of the meaning of these doctrines in terms of their dialectical relationship was, in effect, to allow humanity to create its own religion in the form of an ego-centered paganism, with all of the attendant horrors that such an *ersatz* religion could bring. Commenting on the opening petition of the Lord's Prayer, Guardini once wrote:

Our human nature tries to defend itself against God. The most hidden form
of this defense, its most secret weapon, consists in the inclination of our human
nature to transform the image of God into the likeness of our own image . . .
and so it makes God innocuous. For them there is no longer the encounter,
face, to face, for [the human person] encounters only his [or her] own image
projected into the clouds.[5]

These words were not merely a protest against a line of thinking that was as old
and as commonplace as that found in Feuerbach (along with its economic variant in
Karl Marx or its psychological reduction in Freud's *The Future of an Illusion*). A few
pages later on, commenting on the projected gods of ancient Greece, Guardini strikes a
more ominous note:

We should do well not to dismiss this thought too scornfully; for what assurance
have we that Europe may not return once more to worship "gods"? Though,
to be sure, these gods may be quite different from the gods of antiquity.[6]

It is, then, from the deep center of his faith in God's revelation to us that he
would both articulate his understanding of scripture and set out his understanding of
the culture in which he lived.

In order to extend my point, let me utilize one of Guardini's lesser appreciated
books to illustrate what I mean. In 1963, at the age of 78, Guardini published the fruits
of his long engagement with the psalms, *The Wisdom of the Psalms*. In 1950, Guardini
had been entrusted by the German bishops to provide a German edition of the psalms.
As his biographer noted, this was a labor because Guardini knew no Hebrew and had
to translate from the Latin Vulgate with an eye to the rendition of the psalter done earlier by Martin Buber when Buber was still at Frankfurt's *Judaisches Lehrhaus*.[7]

What interests me about Guardini's meditations on the psalms, born from both
his scholarly labors and his lifelong engagement with them in the liturgy, is both what
he does not consider and, on the positive side, how he approaches the psalms with his
own peculiar hermeneutic. What he does not say, in brief, is anything about the "higher"
criticism that had been produced in Germany and elsewhere about the *Sitz in Leben*,
literary characteristics, distant origins and canonical history of the psalter. If Guardini
knew of the pioneering labors of the biblical scholars Gunkel and Mowinckel, he seems
to have known of them only to the extent that their labors had entered into the conventional wisdom of the time.[8] He does not engage in any sustained dialogue with them
either as a friend or as a polemicist.

Fair enough. Guardini, with his literary, liturgical, spiritual and pastoral concerns, was not doing technical exegesis. At the same time, however, *The Wisdom of the Psalms* was not merely pious eisegesis either. In fact, a careful reading of that book shows that the fundamental poles of Guardini's worldview — creation and revelation — are the twin lenses both through which he reads the psalter and from which he mounts his critique of culture. *The Wisdom of the Psalms,* in short, is an excellent text for understanding how Guardini read scripture from a sapiential stance: through the eyes of faith.

The Wisdom of the Psalms does not survey the entire psalter. Guardini singles out individual psalms in order to offer an extended comment. What is striking about his procedure is the way in which he pulls together, in a single discourse, the ancient poetry with its revelatory voice and the modern temperament, which he hopes to illuminate in a critical and theological fashion.

Commenting on Psalm 148, in which the full panoply of the world is called upon to praise God, he notes — shrewdly, it seems to me — that thinkers of the last four centuries would think of nature when they read that psalm and that nature is something which "gets in the way."[9] But, he goes on to note, the psalm does not speak about "nature," which is an essentially abstract word, alien to the Hebrew poet. Psalm 148 speaks of creation, and "creation restores the world to God's hand." The human task, then — and here Guardini betrays his essentially Bonaventurean cast of mind — is "to translate into words of praise the essential praise that lies in all things." With almost sleight of hand, Guardini displaces nature as being at issue in the psalm to advance a far deeper truth: What is, in all of its singularity, comes from God.

Guardini sees a great danger in forgetting that truth. The modern era is so insistent on "nature" that it can become the bounded horizon of all that a person knows and from within which a person operates. Guardini once wrote that

> so genuine is the world's reality that it can give the appearance of being independent of God. . . . In this life the scales of reality are deceptive, and to reach a conviction of God's sovereignty is a triumph of faith only now and then borne out by inner experience.[10]

The shift from "nature" to "creation" is, in effect, the Guardinian ploy to negate abstractions in order to stay in the more concrete terms of revelation, where the leading concepts find their root in the specificities of events, persons, mighty deeds and, ultimately, in that most concrete of expressions, the Word made flesh.

In a second essay on that same psalm, Guardini writes a striking passage that expresses his deepest conviction about the intertwined doctrines of creation and revelation to which I alluded earlier. He sees the whole litany of the world's dynamism, set out in Psalm 148, as giving evidence of the "solidity, reality, dependability, which every element of creation produces. And in a deeper sense the fact that no mythical demonic power of destruction prevails over the existence of the world."[11]

However much Guardini refers back to demonic forces or destructive patterns (how could he not, having lived through the era of National Socialism), his conviction about the essential goodness of the created world never wavers. Meditating on Psalm 104 (Vulgate 103), Guardini notes the "joy of God in creating" of which the psalmist speaks; of that same psalmist Guardini says that he and all Old Testament believers viewed the world not scientifically or aesthetically, but "prophetically, as a countenance through which God looks at him; God who dwells in light inaccessible."[12]

Let me not be misunderstood. Guardini did not think the psalmist inspired because his poetry pointed to creation alone as a revelation. Rather, Guardini detected something deeper in the psalmist: a longing for yet more intimacy with the Lord of creation. For the modern person it is not enough merely to face creation; to accept a creator demands a *metanoia* of thought. As Guardini says of Psalm 63 (Vulgate 62),

> The psalmist wishes to have communion with [God], not to sink into the primordial foundation of the world or to be dissolved in the strains of existence,
> but to have communion in the dignity of a free person.[13]

In short, Guardini shies away from any all-engrossing nature mysticism that would overwhelm the right of the individual to his or her authentic capacity as a free person.

There is a final point about Guardini's meditation on the psalms that is worth mentioning. In a line that seems almost *en passant,* Guardini undercuts the most telling objection of modern culture in respect to God, namely, that the embrace of creation/revelation may merely be a projection of our own needs onto the cold universe. It may well be, Guardini concedes, that we project, as rationalism says, our own character and emotions on divinity, but he says, "Actually the situation is reversed. Man himself becomes like the divinity in which he believes. And if he does not believe in any [divinity] then it is this nothingness which determines his inmost being."[14]

One can read Guardini's volume on the psalms in the light of a book he published some years earlier on someone who had that *metanoia* of thought which Guardini found absolutely necessary for the believer: Blaise Pascal.

Why would Pascal attract the attention of Guardini? He was hardly a writer that academic theologians found of interest. The clue, I think, is to be found in the persons that Guardini had always found interesting; they form a line that goes back to

Socrates and Augustine and include such modern figures as a lonesome outsider like Søren Kierkegaard, a questioner like Ivan Karamazov or even a titanic figure like Nietzsche — all figures who drew comment from Guardini.

(As an aside to this discussion, I wonder who Guardini would be reading today were he still holding forth from his cathedra. The Russian poets such as Mandelstam and those who have come to us after the fall of the Marxist state? The magic realists? Postmodern writers like Borges, perhaps? Holocaust writers like Primo Levi? Who?)

Guardini's study of Pascal is straightforward enough, but why he wrote on Pascal is announced early, and it is important for my purpose of seeing him as a sapiential theologian. Guardini prefaces his study of Pascal with a series of questions: What happens when a person believes? Not only when a person is a searcher or a seeker after faith but, more radically, when one deeply commits to belief in the full and distinct meaning of the term? And, following on that, two profound issues: What is the structure of the human consciousness based on such belief? How does a life determined by such belief realize itself?[15]

Note the way Guardini frames the issue; it is basically this: What difference does it make when a person says, within the world of the church, *Credo*? It is an issue that he would take up with his study of the young Augustine, which, interestingly enough, was published in the same year as his book on Pascal (1935).

A close reading of *Pascal for Our Time* reveals why Guardini makes this inquiry of Pascal: Pascal was on the cusp of our world, or as Guardini phrases it, "modern consciousness is there but that which preceded it had not yet disappeared."[16] Thus, Guardini recognizes that one can look back beyond Pascal and see old apologetics, or forward to see him, as many have, as the forerunner of a kind of existentialism represented by Søren Kierkegaard and Fydor Dostoevski.

Furthermore, Pascal was a person of science who had a profound religious experience, an experience that permitted him to make two distinctions which, even if he had done nothing else, would make him famous in the intellectual religious history of the West: He articulated the difference between *esprit de la geometrie* and *esprit de la finesse,* and he proclaimed the chasm between the "God of the philosophers" and the "God of Abraham, Isaac, and Jacob" in his *Memorial* of November 23, 1654.

In both of those instances, one can see Guardini's principle of *der Gegensätze* — a kind of dialectical tension of opposites in which the opposing poles are mutually corrected: the elegant intellectual clarity of geometry polished by the refined sensibility of *finesse* and the rational rigor of the god of the philosophers enlarged and — dare I use the word — deconstructed by the living God of the Patriarchs. Precisely because

Guardini is a theologian for whom revelation is the shaping force of experience, he would judge even Pascal's "philosophical" argument for the existence of God (the famous "wager") as only the "gaining of a first footing on the reality of God."[17]

Just as Guardini queries the psalms to look beyond and behind them to the revelatory voice of God, so he sees in Pascal a powerful person, shaped and grasped by deep faith, pushing the limits of reason to something deeper while yet not abandoning his reason. That is why Guardini calls the Kierkegaard of the *Philosophical Fragments* as a witness to what Pascal stood for: "Reason cannot advance beyond this point and yet it cannot refrain its paradoxicalness from arriving at this limit and occupying itself forthwith."[18]

What Guardini tried to do from his own vantage point bears a close resemblance to what many think theology ought to be doing in the future: bringing spirituality and systematic (or for that matter, moral) theology into closer collaboration.

What one sees in Guardini in the few instances I have cited is a theologian who inserts the testimony of religious experience into the field of theological reflection. In that sense his writings look much more like what we could today call "spirituality" as opposed to "systematic theology." I do not say that to classify him as a "spiritual" writer as opposed to a theologian but to note that what Guardini tried to do from his own vantage point bears a close resemblance to what many think theology ought to be doing in the future: bringing spirituality and systematic (or for that matter, moral) theology into closer collaboration.

The attempt to draw the fields of spirituality and theology closer together is one of the more prominent subjects of study in our day. Guardini cannot serve as a fully adequate model for that enterprise because our time demands a willingness both to come to grips with what has happened since the *aggiornamento* brought about by Vatican II and to enter into the ongoing debate about the emerging field(s) of spirituality. As Philip Sheldrake and others have pointed out, one cannot articulate spirituality as a field by repeating slogans from the past. What is required is an advance beyond what once was called "spiritual" theology.[19]

Theology and Spirituality: The Search for Wisdom

In what ways can we learn from Guardini how that task should be undertaken? In the first instance, Guardini never accepted a bifurcation between the reality of religious experience as it wells up from faith and his duty as an intellectual to think about and be critical of what he accepted. It was those twin realities that led him to the great religious geniuses and authentic poets to query and argue with them. It was their insistence on the primacy of religious experience that drew his attention. That permitted him, for the most part, to do theology without any narrow articulation of theological truths into tight propositional statements.

The great challenge, of course, is not to submerge the reality of the Other, encountered as revelation, into the subjective experience of the believer. These two poles must be kept in tension with the power of the Other exercising a prophetic critique on personal experience. Only with that sense of God do we avoid falling into childish dependency or the confines of the "scientific" worldview or, what is worse, the "sense of mission of the exceptional person." Otherness is the criterion that judges the tendency to self-sufficiency or megalomania.[20]

In 1965, at the age of 80, during the heady days of the Council, Guardini still held fast to that truth and expressed it powerfully in a little book, *The Church of the Lord,* which he wrote to complement *The Church and the Catholic,* written in 1922:

> The way to Truth, then, cannot be to "seek God," as we like to say merely through our own experience and our own thought. For if the seeker pictures God in this way and establishes a relationship with him, he really remains with himself and holds fast to himself — only in a more subtle and more closed binding manner than if he declared openly, "I do not want anything to do with God; I am sufficient for myself."[21]

Second, only a theologian who roots his or her reflection in a deep center of faith and who works from that center will have the courage and the willingness to reach out to reflect on the spirit of the age with anything approximating biblical optics. A writer such as Guardini stands as a prophetic alternative to those theologians who have allowed their work to become so academically rarefied that they cannot speak beyond the narrow limits of an academic specialty. This is not to denigrate the difficult task of systematic theology. It is to say that theology will lose its savor to the degree that its audience is only that of the seminar room or of interest solely to tenure and promotion review boards.

Theology at its best speaks from the lecture hall to the church and to the world, and it speaks with deep conviction and from a profound center of faith. That may well mean that much of the theologian's work is time-bound and done on an *ad hoc* basis.[22] That is certainly true of Guardini's work; it is a risk that the theologian takes willingly because the theologian reflects in his or her own present for the needs of his or her time. Only if the insights take on depth do they reach to future ages.

The theologian also writes in the context of, and many times *against,* the predominant culture. Guardini's fascination with creation, for instance, must be seen against some powerful destablizing features of his own time, everything from the uncertainty principle of Heisenberg to the instability seen in nature as successive cultural movements (I have in mind both cubism and the expressionism so popular in Weimar culture) that made the phenomenal world so fluid and protean to the human mind.

At the same time, we should not be inattentive to the time-bound character and the flaws of past thinkers, even such a thinker as Guardini. The recent English-language publication of *Letters from Lake Como* seems an innocently uncritical work.[23] Guardini's somewhat romantic musings about his natal land and his worries about the impact of technology on the landscape seem, when compared with the writings, say, of Ignazio Silone in the early 1930s (e.g., *Fontamara* and *Pane e Vino*), like an exercise in sentimentalism, indeed in *Weltschmerz.* As they say: Even Homer nods.

Nonetheless, Guardini, like Thomas Merton, was a sapiential thinker. He thought, taught and wrote from a deep center of faith without fear as he faced his world — a world shaped by the constrictions of anti-modernism in his own Catholic community and forged in the horrors of two world wars. He died a few years after the great change brought about by the Second Vatican Council. He maintained to the end a sure conviction about the seriousness of his task, and that assurance may be his greatest legacy to us. He did not repeat the slogans of the past, and so he invites us not to repeat the slogans of his own day either.

Guardini expressed the ever-new and ever-old theological task so well in a prayer he once composed that I will let his words stand as a finale to this reflection:

> Give me great seriousness in all that concerns faith. Teach me to see what it
> needs to exist and be fruitful. Let me know its strength and also its weakness.
> If with the passing of time my feeling should change and with it the human
> form but not the divine content of my faith, then teach me to understand that
> change. Grant that in the tests it will bring I will stand firm, so that my faith
> may gain strength and maturity as you, O Ruler of All Life, have so ordained
> it. Amen.[24]

Endnotes

1. I have made the case for Merton as a theologian in this sense in "Thomas Merton as Theologian: An Appreciation," in the Thomas Merton Symposium published in *The Kentucky Review* 7 (1987): 90–97.

2. "Karl Rahner: A Portrait," in idem, *The Content Of Faith: The Best of Karl Rahner's Theological Writings,* trans. Harvey D. Egan (New York: Crossroad, 1992), 11–12.

3. Rahner, *Content of Faith,* 9. Lehmann further says that by the time Rahner took his chair the age of chairs in "worldviews" was already done.

4. Elio Guerierro, *Hans Urs von Balthasar* (Milano: Paoline, 1991), 26 et passim, shows the dependence at length. Von Balthasar would pay due tribute to his old mentor's work in his book *Romano Guardini,* soon to be available in an English translation by Albert K. Wimmer.

5. Romano Guardini, *The Lord's Prayer,* trans. Isabel McHugh (New York: Pantheon, 1958), 27.

6. Guardini, *The Lord's Prayer,* 29. Guardini wrote those words in the early 1930s, which gives them a special pungency.

7. Hanna-Barbara Gerl, *Romano Guardini* (Mainz: Matthias Grünewald, 1985), 348.

8. The crucial German scholarship on the psalms is outlined in Brevard Child, *Introduction to the Old Testament as Scripture* (Philadelphia: Fortress, 1979), 504–25. Hermann Gunkel (d. 1932) and Sigmund Mowinckel (d. 1967) used form criticism in their foundational studies on the psalms.

9. Romano Guardini, *The Wisdom of the Psalms,* trans. by Stella Lange (Chicago: Regnery, 1968), 61–70.

10. Romano Guardini, *The Faith and Modern Man,* trans. Charlotte E. Forsyth (New York: Pantheon, 1952), 48.

11. Guardini, *The Wisdom of the Psalms,* 74.

12. Ibid., 56.

13. Ibid., 119.

14. Ibid., 31

15. Romano Guardini, *Pascal for Our Time,* trans. Brian Thompson (New York: Herder and Herder, 1966). His estimation of Pascal was not uncritical. Guardini thought him lacking in human sympathy and rigid; his criticisms of Kierkegaard, whom he cites in this work, are similar.

16. Ibid., 10.

17. Ibid., 152.

18. Ibid., 153, citing Kierkegaard.

19. Concerning the differences between spiritual theology and spirituality, see Philip Sheldrake, *Spirituality & History: Questions of Interpretation and Method* (New York: Crossroad, 1992), 49 et passim.

20. See Guardini, *The Faith and Modern Man,* 63.

21. Romano Guardini, *The Church of the Lord,* trans. Stella Lange (Chicago: Regnery, 1966), 60–61.

22. Von Balthasar argued that Guardini's work is probably not amenable to systematic treatment because so much of what he wrote was either for the occasion or a "redoing" of earlier, more schematic studies. I would not challenge that judgment. My point is that underneath the diversity are some basic convictions from which the sprawling nature of his work derives. In that sense, he is much like Merton, who also defies any systematic expression of his "thought." See Hans Urs von Balthasar, *Romano Guardini* (Munich: Kösel, 1970).

23. Romano Guardini, *Letters from Lake Como,* trans. Geoffrey W. Bromiley (Grand Rapids: William B. Eerdmans, 1994).

24. Romano Guardini, *Prayers from Theology,* trans. Richard Newnham (New York: Herder and Herder, 1959), 12.

Chapter Six

Romano Guardini's View of Liturgy: A Lens for Our Time

Kathleen Hughes, RSCJ

My approach to this sixth chapter shifted somewhere in the middle of my study. I can best describe this shift by referring to the art of translation. On the one hand, I could tell you what Guardini said about liturgy. I could even tell you what other people said he said and how other people assessed what he said. I could, in other words, render a fairly literal translation of this man's contribution to the liturgical movement in this century and in what ways I think he may have influenced the work of the Liturgical Preparatory Commission of Vatican II (of which he was a member) and, ultimately, the *Constitution on the Sacred Liturgy.*

But having met a man unapologetically captivated by the liturgy, and having discovered how remarkably familiar are the issues he addresses, I have decided that my translation of Guardini on liturgy should employ the principles of dynamic equivalence. I will present to you, often in his words, what I have come to believe he would say *today* were he alive in this new age of the church's life and if he had this platform for his remarks.

The following is an overview of what I will consider:

First, I will begin with Guardini's famous query: Are we capable of a genuine liturgical act? I will discuss what's involved in such an act, what predispositions one must develop and the possible hindrances there are within us and around us.

Second, I will explore the dangers of the liturgical movement as Guardini identified them. The same dangers that surfaced more than 50 years ago are with us still, though their concrete manifestations differ with each new age.

Finally, and very briefly, I shall take up a number of Guardini's particular liturgical preoccupations as they intersect with the needs of today.

In keeping with the style of Guardini, as well as with his substance, I will begin with a reflection on symbol[1] and end, as his lectures so often concluded, with a prayer.[2]

Are We Capable of a Genuine Liturgical Act?

As I begin to reflect with you on our capacity to engage in the liturgical act, on what it would look like and on why it's so elusive, I believe an experience is in order. The "liturgical act" begins and ends with the sign of the cross. Therefore, I invite you to still your mind and your heart, join stillness to composure — what Guardini called "sacred bearing" — read these words and, when you choose, sign yourself with the mark of Christ's cross:

> When we cross ourselves, let it be a real sign of the cross. Instead of a small cramped gesture that gives no notion of its meaning, let us make a large unhurried sign, from forehead to breast, from shoulder to shoulder, consciously feeling how it includes the whole of us, our thoughts, our attitudes, our body and soul, every part of us, how it consecrates and sanctifies us. It does so because it is the sign of the universe and the sign of our redemption. On the cross, Christ redeemed [human]kind. By the cross he sanctifies [us] to the last shred and fibre of [our] being. . . . Think of these things when you make the sign of the cross. It is the holiest of all signs. Make a large cross, taking time, thinking what you do. Let it take in your whole being — body, soul, mind, will, thoughts, feelings, your doing and not doing — and by signing [your whole being] with the cross, strengthen and consecrate the whole in the strength of Christ, in the name of the triune God.[3]

Now let's consider, along with Guardini, what we do when we sign ourselves with the mark of Christ's cross.

To make the sign of the cross, the sign that Guardini called the simplest and holiest of all signs, and to make it with an awareness of both *what* we are doing and *with whom* we are doing it, is the beginning of the liturgical act or, more accurately, the beginning of a whole world of acts that constitute our service of God, our liturgy. Everything we do — our entering, our being present, our kneeling, sitting and standing, our listening, seeing and speaking, our processing, our reception of the body and blood of Christ, our leaving to love and serve the Lord — all of it is divine service. But "this is so only when all we do 'overflows' from the awareness of a collected heart and the mind's attentiveness."[4]

Throughout his life, much that Guardini preached, taught and wrote about the liturgy revolved around the conditions for the possibility of such awareness and attentiveness. Four years before his death, in April 1964, just a few months after the promulgation of the *Constitution on the Sacred Liturgy* and when Guardini was unable to attend the Third German Liturgical Congress, he wrote an open letter to the Congress that placed his lifelong preoccupation on both their agenda and the subsequent agendas of most serious liturgists.

The phrase "active participation" implies participation in the whole of the ritual event to such an extent that one is joined to Jesus Christ, dead and risen, and so to the priestly work of Christ, who stands before the throne of grace interceding on behalf of the world.

How, he asked, are we to set about the task of liturgical renewal? So much needed to be done in the wake of the Council's decisions. Historical, liturgical and pastoral studies had to be completed. Ritual and textual problems and questions were inevitable. The machinery of reform — the committees, the production of new rites, the implementation — all of it was staggering. And none of it, for Guardini, was the central problem. In his words:

> The question is whether the wonderful opportunities now open to the liturgy
> will achieve their full realization; whether we shall be satisfied with just remov-
> ing anomalies, taking new situations into account, giving better instruction
> on the meaning of ceremonies and liturgical vessels or whether we shall relearn
> a forgotten way of doing things and recapture lost attitudes.[5]

Are we capable of a liturgical act? The essence of liturgy is encounter with God through Christ Jesus. The phrase "active participation" implies participation in the whole of the ritual event to such an extent that one is joined to Jesus Christ, dead and risen, and so to the priestly work of Christ, who stands before the throne of grace interceding on behalf of the world. Are we capable of this? Can we relearn a forgotten way of doing things? Can we recapture lost attitudes, attitudes toward God, toward those around us, and toward ourselves? Can we approach the liturgy and engage its sights and sounds, its words and gestures?

> The more we think about these long-familiar things the clearer does their mean-
> ing grow. Things we have done thousands of times, if we will only look into
> them more deeply, will disclose to us their beauty. If we listen, they will speak.
>
> After their meaning has been revealed to us, the next step is to enter
> upon our inheritance and make what we have long possessed really our own.

We must learn how to see, how to hear, how to do things the right way. Such a learning-by-looking, growing-by-learning, is what matters. Regarded any other way these things keep their secret. They remain dark and mute. Regarded thus, they yield to us their essential nature, that nature which formed them to their outward shapes. Make trial for yourself. The most commonplace everyday objects and actions hide matters of deepest import. Under the simplest exteriors lie the great mysteries.[6]

What are the preconditions for entering into this mystery? First, Guardini suggests, despite all the distractions around us and within us, we must learn the art of stillness, which is absolutely indispensable for the liturgical act. "Stillness is the tranquility of the inner life; the quiet at the depths of its hidden stream. It is a collected, total presence, a being 'all there,' receptive, alert, ready."[7] And stillness, to be effective, must be joined to inward composure. For "silence overcomes noise and talk; composure is the victory over distractions and unrest. Silence is the quiet of a person who could be talking; composure is the vital, dynamic unity of an individual who could be divided by his [or her] surroundings, tossed to and fro by the myriad happenings of every day."[8] Only when composure has been realized is attention possible, and so, too, the liturgical act. And finally, to stillness and composure add "the ability to play," for

The soul must learn to abandon, at least in prayer, the restlessness of purposeful activity; it must learn to waste time for the sake of God, and to be prepared for the sacred game with sayings and thoughts and gestures, without always immediately asking "why?" and "wherefore?" It must learn not to be continually yearning to do something, to attack something, to accomplish something useful, but to play the divinely ordained game of the liturgy in liberty and beauty and holy joy before God.[9]

Ultimately, the liturgical act that Guardini proposes is an act of contemplation, begun in stillness, composure and a spirit of play before God. "Active participation," the phrase that captured the imagination and gathered up the hopes of countless men and women in the liturgical movement of this century is, paradoxically, an act of attentive and contemplative surrender. When we are engaged in the genuine liturgical act, we are not simply saying things, nor simply watching things, nor even just doing things: We are saying and watching and doing attentively, as whole human persons, together with others, forming one body giving glory to God. When we are engaged in the genuine liturgical act, we are just that — *engaged!* Personal contemplative engagement is the heart of the liturgical act.

Are we capable of it? At least some would suggest that contemplation is a lost art, virtually impossible in the noise and the haste and amid the endless distractions of our society. Is it more difficult for us than our ancestors in the faith? Perhaps! But Robert Bellah and his colleagues, in their latest book, *The Good Society,* have made a strong case for the urgent recovery of contemplation. They call contemplation "paying attention," and they suggest that one way of defining democracy is to call it a system in which people actively attend to what is significant and concern themselves with the larger meaning of things. As they observe:

> Few things in life are more important. For paying attention is how we use our psychic energy, and how we use our psychic energy determines the kind of self we are cultivating, the kind of person we are learning to be. When we are giving our full attention to something, when we are really attending, we are calling on all our resources of intelligence, feeling, and moral sensitivity.[10] . . .
>
> If we are going to be the kind of persons we want to be, and live the kind of lives we want to live, then attention and not distraction is essential. Concerns that are most deeply personal are closely connected with concerns that are global in scope. We cannot be the caring people whom our children need us to be and ignore the world they will have to live in. We cannot hide the fact that without effective democratic intervention and institution-building the world economy might accelerate in ways that will tear our lives apart and destroy the environment. Moral discourse is essential in the family; it is also essential in the world. There is no place to hide. "Distracted from distraction by distraction" is how T. S. Eliot characterized our situation. It is time to pay attention.[11]

So while some might be inclined to think of "a contemplative attitude" as a quaint anachronism and certainly impossible to achieve in our age, the social commentators who wrote *The Good Society* suggest that contemplation, or attentiveness, is an art we must relearn, an attitude of heart essential for the very survival of civil society. How much more so is it an attitude essential for the survival of the liturgy!

Why does it seem so difficult to attain? Guardini names three enemies of contemplative engagement: habit, sentimentality and human nature.

Habit is the result of that "fundamental spiritual law that every impression exhausts itself. All life is a perpetual becoming, but also a perpetual perishing; thus an impression starts out strong, gains in strength, lasts for a while and then fades."[12] In the end, indifference begins to erode participation.

At first fleetingly, then ever more prolonged and powerfully, the feeling of monotony creeps in. "I know all that. I know exactly what words will follow every move." When, in addition, the same priest appears at the same altar over a long period, officiating in the same manner with his unchanging personal peculiarities and shortcomings, a veritable crisis of boredom and weariness can overcome us. We no longer "get anything out of it," hardly know why we still go.[13]

The second enemy of contemplative engagement is *sentimentality:*

To put it bluntly, sentimentality is essentially the desire to be moved: by loneliness or delight, sorrow or dread; by greatness and exaltedness or weakness and helplessness — somehow to be moved. . . . Sentimentality is a half sentiment, a spiritual softness tinged with sensuality. . . . For the sentimental believer, participation in Mass is extremely difficult. He [or she] finds the sacred act neither comforting nor edifying, but austere, coldly impersonal, almost forbidding.[14]

There is absolutely nothing of the sentimental in the celebration of the eucharist unless it is manipulated by sentimental ministers using words dripping with feeling, exciting imagery, moving dialogue and the like, and turning the celebration of liturgy into a kind of passion play. Such is antithetical to the nature of the liturgical act.

Finally, because original sin is alive and well, *human nature* itself is at odds with contemplative engagement:

God's sacred act is planted in human imperfection. Celebrated by a priest for whom the liturgy is really alive, its words and gestures are convincing; by one who is not immersed in the spirit of the liturgy, they are apt to appear forced and unnatural. Then there are all the private, little shortcomings of speech and bearing and movement which can be so distracting. The same is true of the congregation. It too can be understanding or indifferent, can actively participate or merely allow events to take their course. It can be educated to the celebration of the Mass and really understand; but it can also passively watch the ceremony unwind, an accepted tradition, day after day and Sunday after Sunday. It can enter into the sacred action or remain outside, carrying on its private devotion with all the varying shades of mood that every variable human life contains.[15]

In reflecting on the liturgical act and what makes it difficult, add to habit, sentimentality and human nature the cult of instant intimacy, which sets up impossible expectations in our assemblies; the dualism of mind and body, which undermines whole-person engagement; the entertainment model of participation, which dulls our sensibilities; and individualism, which vitiates what is essentially a corporate experience. Furthermore, sometimes those of us who have the responsibility of teaching and training others, as well as those of us who are engaged in the continued work of reform and renewal of worship at the diocesan and the parochial levels, are the worst enemies of the genuine liturgical act. Guardini was aware of such dangers from within the movement. To these, explicitly, we turn.

Dangers of Liturgical Renewal

A collection of studies published in 1963 in commemoration of the sixtieth anniversary of Pius X's movement-launching Motu Proprio, *Tra le sollecitudini,* included a contribution from Romano Guardini titled "Some Dangers of the Liturgical Revival." Some commentators have wondered about the timing of this excursus on the weaknesses and dangers of the renewal in the same year that the *Constitution on the Liturgy* was being debated, refined and promulgated. In fact, Guardini's contribution to the anniversary collection originated as a letter *in defense* of the liturgical movement, written in 1940 to a rather skittish German hierarchy to head them off at the pass.

With apology for employing labels always open to distortion, Guardini identified the dangers of rubricism, activism, dilettantism and conservatism. Apparent to anyone picking up this material is that the dangers Guardini first identified in the liturgical revival of 1940, and which were sufficiently apposite that they could be published again in 1963, have continued to haunt the reform and renewal of the liturgy in 1994. Let's look at them in turn.

First, *rubricism.* We often associate rubricism with that approach to liturgy, prior to the Council, which exaggerated the exact manner of carrying out particular ceremonies and which left a presider open to the commission of a variety of sins, both venial and mortal, if he did not comport himself precisely according to the various rubrical directives. But I believe a different kind of rubricism is alive and well today. Guardini described rubricism as a tendency to attribute to the liturgy an importance that it does not possess,[16] and he seemed to limit rubricism to the first stage of liturgical revival.

We know better. Rubricism speaks today in the language of always and never; rubricism treats the liturgy as a performance rather than as a prayer; rubricism turns upside down the gospel teaching that the Sabbath is made for humankind and not vice versa; rubricism creates chancel prancers and makes others despise the whole effete world of liturgical renewal. It is the tendency on the part of some to so exaggerate one and only one way of performing various ceremonies that it even gave rise to a comparison of liturgists with terrorists. Vatican II did not eliminate rubricism; it simply enlarged its horizon.

Activism is a second danger to liturgical renewal. It is a tendency to so emphasize the church's mission that "prayer, the undemanding absorption of self in eternal things, the sacred worship before God's countenance [is regarded as] a waste of time . . . , pointless . . . , superfluous."[17] If activism does not undermine liturgy altogether, it treats it pragmatically, refashioning the liturgy in order to drive home whatever particular justice issue might be pressing. Activism expects quick, immediate, even numerically tangible results.

The relationship of liturgy and just living is a perennial question, or as one of my colleagues phrases it: "What do all those Masses do for us, anyway?" Activism flies in the face of liturgy as play. It makes of worship a purposeful rather than a purposeless activity, yet "when the liturgy is rightly regarded, it cannot be said to have a purpose, because it does not exist for the sake of humanity, but for the sake of God."[18] Activism wants results, not the slow, imperceptible but radical reordering of our minds and hearts that takes place over a lifetime.

Dilettantism is the third danger Guardini identified and, in my judgment, it is a particularly rampant danger in our day. Guardini notes that movements which begin slowly and in relative obscurity often reach a point where there is a sudden leap into the awareness of the general public. It happens when movements pick up steam and begin to capture the corporate imagination. A popular movement is good news and bad news. On the one hand, the fundamental "rightness" of the movement appears to be legitimated by numbers, but on the other hand, there is the danger of "hasty, disjointed and insufficiently experienced action," when proponents without grounding, ability or prudence take over. As Guardini pointed out:

> Many of those who ventured into this field had no conception of the amount
> of historical, theological, philological and musical knowledge required to bring
> out more clearly the essence of a symbolic action or to compose a tune which
> is both in the tradition of plainchant and truly part of the life of the people.[19]

Dilettantism, I suppose, is unavoidable. A little knowledge is a dangerous thing. Workshops, study days, even degree programs have made dabblers of many in the assembly who now rewrite texts, rearrange furniture and redistribute roles with a certain abandon but with the best of intentions. Sometimes changes are unconnected, sometimes arbitrary. No matter. The end result is too often a plethora of ill-conceived and confusing experiments with the structure and forms of the liturgy, which only postpones the day of engagement in the liturgical act.[20]

The fourth danger is the inevitable reaction to dilettantism, *conservatism:*

> Liturgical conservatives felt keenly the dangers I have just set out. They saw that rubricism did not take into account the real nature of parish life, while dilettantism brought the danger of confusion and arbitrary action. In opposition to activism, they stressed the necessity to build upon the inner basic religious life rather than on external methods and aids. In all this they were right, but they fell into the danger of rejecting anything to which they were not accustomed. As far as they are concerned, "traditional" equals "good," and "new" equals "irreligious."[21]

Few have not felt the repercussions of "conservatism" in our day. Posture, liturgical ministries and who performs them, principles of translation, design of space, choice of music — no element of the event of worship escapes the conservative critique. And everywhere, it would seem, there lurks the specter of heresy!

Four dangers: rubricism, activism, dilettantism and conservatism; four extremes in the liturgical revival; four inevitable tendencies in any movement of such import when so many people of such evident good will but such differing theologies, ecclesiologies, spiritualities, pastoral sensitivities, cultural perceptions, ritual insights and liturgical training all get into the act. It would be easiest at this juncture to call a halt to the reform of liturgy before the renewal has even begun, but that is the final danger of which Guardini warns us, the danger of administrative short-circuit:[22]

> It is natural that the ecclesiastical authorities should take steps against arbitrary innovations, justified neither by office nor by ability. It is more than just that they should demand and require actions from their priests, especially from the younger ones, and that the latter should have to learn before they act on their own account. On the other hand a great deal depends on them, not to withdraw their confidence from those who have been working on these matters for so long with seriousness and feelings of responsibility, but to protect them from attacks which call in question their convictions and their work.[23]

An obvious case in point is that of the attack, often vicious, against the current work of the International Commission on English in the Liturgy (ICEL) in revising the sacramentary and the disarray and inability of the National Conference of Catholic

Bishops to put an end to the spurious charges that are being leveled against the work of ICEL. There are, furthermore, rumblings that Rome is rescinding permission to use the New Revised Standard Version of the Bible (NRSV) in liturgical proclamation, that the 1969 "Instruction on Translation" is being augmented to cover (read: resolve once and for all) questions of inclusive language, that inculturation of liturgy is still being interpreted in extrinsicist fashion, that worship offices will continue to be closed for want of funding and personnel, that roles — despite legislation to the contrary — will remain closed to women. The litany could go on and on.

Order at any price is a great temptation in our day. But the imposition of order will put an end, once and for all, to good and important endeavors. And at the same time, as Guardini pleaded with the German bishops, so, too, for today:

> What any liturgical work needs is time. There is a lot to do, the problems are great. To make progress, much theoretical knowledge, much practical knowledge, manifold linguistic and musical abilities are necessary. So we ask for patience. We know that it is asking a great deal to leave things in the balance. But otherwise no good can come of it; and measures which would hinder a work, already several decades old, from yielding matured fruits, would be far worse than any temporary uncertainty.[24]

A Few Particular Issues

Guardini once delineated the several phases of the liturgical movement: the restorative, the academic, the practical, and — my word, not his — the transformative.[25] It is high time the fourth phase begins, infusing new life into the liturgy and into those who engage in it.[26] Allow me, in the space remaining at my disposal, simply to note for you some of Guardini's chief preoccupations which, in my judgment, remain central to our liturgical agenda.

First, stillness, composure and play are conditions for the possibility of contemplative surrender. We must so desire that engagement with God which surrender makes possible that we will be willing to relearn these forgotten ways of doing things and recapture these lost attitudes.[27]

Second, we must release the symbol power of the liturgy: the sacred signs, the objects, movements, actions, time, space and, above all, the sign-value of one another as co-offerers with Christ. We do this, for the most part, by transparent, non-manipulative ministry.[28]

Third, how we catechize communities and train presiders and other ministers must change. Guardini believed scholarly research was not enough and that it was not possible simply to be told about worship. He was convinced, and I have been persuaded, that the doing of liturgy is absolutely basic, and that only after is it possible to distill theology from experience.[29]

Fourth, reflection on experience, when the experience is that of liturgy, is called *myst-agogical,* a form of preaching that Guardini promoted and whose task is not to elucidate dogma, to edify the mind, or to impart spiritual, aesthetic or "feel-good" emotions but to place the community in contact with the living God. Such preaching must become the norm.[30]

Fifth, each time we assemble for the liturgy, a disparate collection of individuals must be forged into a worshiping community, and for this we need to sacrifice self-sufficiency and independence, develop a widened outlook and foster reciprocal reverence.[31] These are counter-cultural values as urgent today as in Guardini's time.

Sixth, speaking of counter-cultural values, I have been struck by Guardini's unapologetic emphasis on the demands that liturgy places on us and on the necessity of personal sacrifice, asceticism, courage, humility and a score of other virtues. What I get out of liturgy in Guardini's view, is quite incidental; what I put into it is crucial. Are we willing to speak this disturbing word and to accept, ourselves, the exigencies of worship in spirit and in truth?

Minds and hearts will be renewed by the liturgy as we give ourselves over to the action of Christ that is its heart, as we learn contemplative engagement in Christ's one great sacrifice of praise and as we allow the power of the Spirit of God to transform us as surely as the bread and wine.

Conclusion

Many of Guardini's liturgical preoccupations remain central to the agenda of renewal. While the reform of the liturgy is virtually complete, the renewal that it promises has barely begun. Minds and hearts will be renewed by the liturgy as we give ourselves over to the action of Christ that is its heart, as we learn contemplative engagement in Christ's one great sacrifice of praise and as we allow the power of the Spirit of God to transform us as surely as the bread and wine.

And we will avoid the minefield of dangers surrounding the ongoing renewal of the liturgy as we take to heart Guardini's words:

Every Amen remains valueless unless God pronounces it. . . . If it is to be really Amen, then God must speak it. God who is fidelity itself must ground us in fidelity. God who is truth itself must enlighten our minds. God must take hold of us and give us that strength which endures in all the ups and downs of life, and rises again and again when everything threatens to sink.[32]

And so we pray: "Bring the Amen to life within us — as truth deeply rooted; fidelity which does not waver; resolution which does not tire!"[33] Amen.

Endnotes

1. Romano Guardini believed that if the liturgical act is to be taken seriously, we must prepare for it beforehand with the total concentration of mind and heart. His book *Meditations Before Mass* originated as discourses immediately before Mass that prepared the community for a more attentive celebration. *Sacred Signs* is another collection of reflections of the actions and visible objects of worship. It was Guardini's hope that such reflections would carry the mind to the divine meaning behind the visible form.

2. See Romano Guardini, *Prayers from Theology,* trans. Richard Newnham (New York: Herder and Herder, 1956). In this collection are prayers that Guardini offered at the conclusion of lectures in order to move his audience and himself from the thoughts of the lecture to prayer to God. As he noted in the introduction: "Knowledge itself shall lead on into prayer, when truth becomes love."

3. Romano Guardini, *Sacred Signs,* trans. Grace Branham (St. Louis: Pio Decimo Press, 1956), 13–14.

4. Romano Guardini, *Meditations Before Mass,* trans. Elinor Castendyk Briefs (Westminster, Maryland: The Newman Press, 1955), 26.

5. Romano Guardini, "A Letter from Romano Guardini," *Herder Correspondence* 1 (Special Issue, 1964), 24.

6. Guardini, *Sacred Signs,* 33–34.

7. Guardini, *Meditations Before Mass,* 5.

8. Ibid., 15.

9. Romano Guardini, *The Spirit of the Liturgy,* trans. Ada Lane (London: Sheed and Ward, 1937), 106.

10. Robert Bellah et al. (eds.), *The Good Society* (New York: Random House/Vintage Books), 254.

11. Ibid., 275–76.

12. Guardini, *Meditations Before Mass,* 97.

13. Ibid., 98–99.

14. Ibid., 102–103.

15. Ibid., 110.

16. Romano Guardini, "Some Dangers of the Liturgical Revival," in *Unto the Altar,* ed. Alfons Kirchengässner (New York: Herder and Herder, 1963), 13.

17. Ibid., 15.

18. Guardini, *The Spirit of the Liturgy,* 96.

19. Guardini, "Some Dangers of the Liturgical Revival," 17.

20. Aesthetes are particularly contemptuous dilettantes according to Guardini. In *The Spirit of the Liturgy,* he noted: The careworn man who seeks nothing at Mass but the fulfillment of the service which he owes to his God; the busy woman, who comes to be a little lightened of her burden; the many people who, barren of feeling and perceiving nothing of the beauty and splendor of word and sound which surrounds them, but merely seek strength for their daily toil — all these penetrate far more deeply into the essence of the liturgy than does the connoisseur who is busy savoring the contrast between the austere beauty of a Preface and the melodiousness of a Gradual. (p. 109)

21. Guardini, *Unto the Altar,* 18.

22. Cuthbert Johnson, OSB, one of the staff of the Congregation for Worship and Sacraments, cites Guardini's list of dangers in an article titled "On the Eve of the Publication of 'Sacrosanctum Concilium'," *Notitiae* 18 (August – September, 1982): 413 – 17. But when it comes to the last danger, "the danger of ecclesiastical short-circuit," Johnson softens the language considerably and speaks of a "caution to those in authority against seeking a facile solution to these problems" (p. 416). Calling a halt to the reform — ecclesiastical short-circuit — is a very real danger precisely at the hands of the Congregation that Johnson represents.

23. Guardini, *Unto the Altar,* 20.

24. Ibid., 21.

25. Guardini, "A Letter," 25 – 26.

26. For a selection of representative writings by the leaders of the liturgical movement, see Kathleen Hughes (ed.), *How Firm a Foundation: Voices of the Early Liturgical Movement* (Chicago: Liturgy Training Publications, 1990).

27. Guardini treats the playfulness of the liturgy as well as its seriousness in *The Spirit of the Liturgy,* 85 – 129.

28. See Guardini, "The Symbolism of the Liturgy," *The Spirit of the Liturgy,* 79 – 84.

29. See Guardini, "Introduction," *Sacred Signs,* 9 – 12.

30. See Guardini, "The Mystagogical Sermon," in *Unto the Altar,* 158 – 69.

31. See Guardini, "The Fellowship of the Liturgy," *The Spirit of the Liturgy,* 37 – 50.

32. Romano Guardini, *The Lord's Prayer,* trans. Isabel McHugh (New York: Pantheon Books, 1958), 123 – 24, passim.

33. Ibid., 125.

Chapter Seven

Encounters with Romano Guardini

Romano Guardini was such a complex, profound personality that if we are to understand his life and work, we must hear about him from those who came into direct contact with him. What follows are four reminiscences concerning Romano Guardini.

I.

Romano Guardini in Berlin

Regina Kuehn

When I met Guardini, I was 13 years old. Thirteen-year-olds raised under political pressure are a different breed from 13-year-olds raised on computer games. I was in my fourth year of high school, a gymnasium with a classical curriculum that begins at age ten. It was run by the Ursulines who — in Europe — are the female version of the Jesuits. The school taught the children of the diplomatic corps. I remember the long limousines and the bodyguards in front of our school building. All of our teachers were at least trilingual; they did not socialize with us students at all.

My situation was different, though; two female teachers formed an alliance with me early on. They trusted me as politically "safe" because my mother had worked for Matthias Erzberger, the head of the Armistice Commission. He was the German diplomat who signed the Versailles Treaty, which would end World War I. Subsequently my mother worked as a night secretary for Chancellor Heinrich Brüning, from whom

Hitler wrested power in 1933. He gave two golden coins to my mother so that she could have her wedding rings made. (I wear one of them.)

Both politicians, Erzberger and Brüning, were devout Catholics — daily communicants, as one used to say. Frequently they worked through the night and then received communion in the morning, together with their staff. Compare this with our White House! It was this connection that became my link to Guardini, as well as my being the speaker for the student body of my school. That meant, among other things, that I would officially greet the Vatican Nuncio to Berlin, Eugenio Pacelli (later Pope Pius XII), who celebrated Mass at our school from time to time. The Nuncio to Berlin was traditionally the dean of the diplomatic corps.

My two teachers took me along to St. Benedict Chapel on Schlüterstrasse for Sunday Mass and introduced me to Guardini. He was interested in my background, and in a moment you will understand why. The Students' Chapel was a large basement room made suitable for celebrating Sunday liturgies. There was a sizable figure of Christ, a metal repoussé work, in back of the free-standing, simple altar, which was surrounded by wooden cubes for seating. The presider's cube closed the circle. Most of us stood, however, because *Sacred Signs* had taught us the significance of this noble gesture. The English language pays full attention to the *virtue* of standing by allowing such phrases as "having a spine" or "being upright" to have a double meaning. We also understood what it meant to be the *circumstantes,* "those standing around the altar."

We became absolutely quiet, and in complete stillness and composure we stood to witness a cosmic event of world-wide consequence in which all of us — each one individually and all of us together — played a part. In the chapel Guardini exemplified the discipline of speech, for example, by not speaking unless one had something to say; and that "something" was either memorable or worth repeating. At times he would even cancel his homily because he had nothing to say. There wasn't anything morally wrong with small talk, according to Guardini, it was just that it took time away from saying something important that was often screaming out to be said. In this context, the use or non-use of words, Guardini was apologetic about having written so many books and articles. He said he would be embarrassed, except that all these things had to be said.

The then – student chaplain and outstanding liturgist, Dr. Johannes Pinsk (who later became our personal friend and presided at our wedding and baptized our children), obliged Guardini to do what was being done in this chapel: to celebrate *versus populum.* Guardini was horrified to think that people would stare at his face while he was praying and watch while he was performing the sacred action. But once he reluctantly agreed, he experienced an unexpected gift. He said, "We all were connected"

("Wir gehörten alle zusammen"). And nothing had changed but *one* simple gesture of *one* man: We did not turn the altar around, we turned the *priest* around. He regretted that he had not faced the people much earlier in his priestly life.

The *missa recitata* was the manner of celebration. All of us were familiar with Latin; this fact alone may tell you that he gathered an elite group around himself. That was his style. It was not that he had no room in his heart and in his mind for people other than the elite, but he personally had no talent to connect with people other than intellectuals. However, because he was an almost scrupulously conscientious priest, he obliged us to take on this task of connecting, each one of us to our particular "circles."

I never heard him remark on the different tasks of ordained and lay people. We were all Gottesvolk, *people of God, with our individual baptismal mission to participate in the "bringing home of the world into Christ's kingdom."*

To me that meant my 500 schoolmates, my parents' political friends and my parish youth groups. Guardini himself did not organize any of the ways of connecting. He laid full responsibility on each member of his circle. I never heard him remark on the different tasks of ordained and lay people. We were all *Gottesvolk,* people of God, with our individual baptismal mission to participate in the *Heimholung der Welt* (the "bringing home of the world into Christ's kingdom").[1] He appealed to each one of us to be an agent (from the Latin *agere,* to act) instead of being forced into the category of "lay," which then was usually understood to mean half as competent as "ordained" and not *really* responsible. To feel called by a man so highly respected and so visibly endowed with a special charisma was a true vocation and an ordination of sorts to restore and guard the sacred.

After my baccalaureate, which marked the closing of our school by the Nazis (our nuns emigrated to Chile), and after my forced time in the Labor Service, I became a student at the State Library of Berlin, the impressive building next to Humboldt University, to prepare for a career as a scientific research librarian. (Over the years, Guardini had found much comfort in the Great Reading Hall of this library, where he regularly prepared himself before his lectures.) Besides studying subjects such as the Dewey decimal system, I took courses from Guardini at the university on Hölderlin and later on Dostoevski and Rilke.

My specialty was to be "the library in the service of the arts." Soon I discovered that the field was much too wide for me to become a well-informed specialist. Guardini invited me to think about architecture and liturgical art, and I began work on my doctoral thesis, in which he guided me. It took on the title, "The Influence of the Liturgical

Movement on the Architecture of Family Homes and Churches" *("Der Einfluß der Litur-gischen Bewegung auf den Haus- und Kirchenbau").* Much of the content of the thesis was composed of theories promoted by Rudolf Schwarz, the architectural genius who had rebuilt Burg Rothenfels into a Catholic youth and worship center. Schwarz had not only built a number of churches that anticipated the post – Vatican II mode but had also built a house for Guardini in Schlachtensee, a southwestern suburb of Berlin. This was the only house Guardini would ever call his home.

Guardini invited me once to his "sanctuary," an unusual honor for a student. Everything in the house was functional, of great simplicity, of the essence of beauty, and an intuitive absence of everything that would distract from the innate nobility of a piece of furniture or art. Everything was in order. He spoke to me about the soul of a house, about words spoken within the walls that would remain and cling to the walls and never again disappear. He spoke about the care one should take to make these lasting words into a shelter where the sacred would want to dwell, where word patterns of kindness, humility, respect and truth could become a grid to holiness, and where culture and sanctity would be synonymous.

I found it difficult to be in his presence. There was no way out; one had no choice but to burn in the fire of his intensity and be totally absorbed. This was the man who drew hundreds of listeners to his daily lectures, so that the use of the Aula Maxima had to be grudgingly granted to him. This was the man of whom audiences spoke with hushed admiration. Never did I hear anyone say of him, as is so common today, "Oh, we just love him," or, "He is a holy person," another present-day term of admiration.

For Guardini's lectures people came in silent concentration. They wanted to be there, to be with him, to be present when he humbly commanded the sacred. He never used "holy language," and even less so, "liturgical jargon," which more often alienates than attracts. His words were harmonious, chosen as if ready to go to print, strong and manly, though spoken with physical effort because of his asthmatic condition.[2] He was a picture of self-discipline. Later we learned that he delivered his lectures with such concentration that, unnoticed by himself, he stood on his toes throughout his one-hour presentations. We also learned that the refined balance of his words, an aesthetic marvel, was not only due to an innate talent but was much rather the result of intense rewriting and polishing.

When in 1939 the Nazis dismissed Guardini from his position at the University of Berlin by forcing him to resign, most students followed him to his evening lectures, sponsored by Catholic Adult Education and the Catholic Women's Alliance *(Katholischer Frauenbund)* at the Jesuit Canisius Church. People braved regular bomb attacks for the unforgettable experience of hearing the truth questioned, examined, reaffirmed and made to shine — an experience as rare then as it is today. Together with his colleague Heinrich Kahlefeld, an Oratorian priest who is buried next to him in Munich, he held his lectures in the framework of a free-styled evening prayer, wearing simple vesture so that he would not offend the many non-Catholics who attended the lecture/prayer service. Kahlefeld was the liturgist who at that time experimented with the Easter Vigil, celebrating it late at night on Saturday rather than at the customary pre-dawn hour on Sunday.

When he was invited to preach at the Protestant Dome in Berlin, Guardini filled the place to the last pew. We had to strain to understand him, because he had a small voice and there was no amplification. When he had finished, he received a long standing ovation, something unthinkable at that time. After a while he addressed the crowd in his usual humble and noble manner, saying one sentence only: "This is the glory of our faith," which invited a second round of applause. Can you sense the political power of a man who dared to preach the truth in the wake of the total collapse of humanity — and this on the opposite end of the same avenue (our Magnificent Mile in Berlin) on which Hitler's palace and its bunker were located?

In the meantime, my two teachers who had introduced me to Guardini and thereby determined my life-long occupation with liturgy and the arts were met with tragic events. Dr. Renate Dessauer's brother was beheaded because he had participated in the unsuccessful attempt on Hitler's life. Dr. Maria Blümel's father, who was the director of the world-famous Pergamon Museum of Antiquity, was dismissed, and as a Catholic was found to be untrustworthy to administer the nation's treasures. Of my twenty-eight classmates, all but one had lost to the war a brother, fiancé, husband or father. To read or discuss Guardini without paying attention to such political events is to lose a hold on his daily reality.

When Guardini decided to leave Berlin because the bomb attacks were affecting his physical and emotional ability to function, and because the government had ordered Berliners not employed in life-securing jobs to leave the city, we were left with a feeling of despair. God had called his prophet away from us and sent him into exile. Together with other students I helped pack his books, which were his comfort and his curse. In the near future, they will be reunited in his house in Mooshausen (Allgäu), which was acquired by the Circle of Guardini Friends (a legal entity) to become in 1995 a museum and library of Guardini treasures and a lecture hall.[3]

II.

Romano Guardini in Munich

Albert K. Wimmer

Initially I was not sure what an occasional visitor to Guardini's lectures like me could contribute to a consideration of this creative theologian's life and work. I am neither a theologian nor a trained philosopher. Ask me — a professor of the German language and literature — about the glottal stop in German or the faculties of the Holy Grail in Wolfram von Eschenbach's *Parzival,* and I would be able to tell you a thing or two. Nevertheless, I will offer a few remembrances from my university years.

I would like to preface my remarks by describing them as something that, in the eyes of the experts, would possibly pass as a study in eclecticism, perhaps even dilettantism. Yet just reminiscing about my studies at the University of Munich from 1958 to 1961 made me realize that my experience was most likely something unique. At the same time, trying to remember a period in my life from over thirty years ago when I was definitely in my formative stage has substantially jogged my memory.

One of the jolts was the recollection of a lecture Martin Heidegger presented in January during the 1958–1959 winter semester on language, with the appropriate Heideggerian subtitle "On Discussing Language as Language in Terms of Language." Or, in his inimitable German:

Die Sprache

als Sprache

zur Sprache

bringen.

I attended Romano Guardini's lectures from 1958 through 1960. At the time, I was a pre-law, history and literature major and frequently sat in on Guardini's Wednesday evening lectures in the Aula Maxima. Actually, he lectured during the dinner hour, and it was certainly to his credit that he rarely failed to fill the hall. The titles of these series of lectures were: "The Structure and Ethics of Christian Existence" (fall 1958), "The Moral Life" (summer 1960) and "History and Eternity" (spring 1961).

To me, Romano Guardini was "a teacher for a day and a subsequent parent for life." I do not recall the origin of this phrase, but it certainly illustrates the way I feel about — please forgive me for this frivolous comparison — the best thing to come out of the city of Verona since Romeo and Juliet.[4]

I walked away from Guardini's lectures with essentially three key recollections that have been permanently inscribed in my mind.

First, there are Guardini's concepts of freedom and being a person of culture (*Kulturmensch*) in combination with insights that have forever shaped my understanding of the relationship between literature and religion.

I can still hear him speaking of being in control and of making use of oneself, of understanding where we come from, why we are living here and where we are going.

He encouraged his listeners to combine these insights with "the ability to break out of the confines of their existence."

Concerning Guardini's definition of Christian freedom: I can still hear him speaking of being in control and of making use of oneself (*über sich verfügen*), of *sich verstehen*, that is, of understanding where it is that we come from, why we are living here and where we are going. He encouraged his listeners to combine these insights with "the ability to break out of the confines of their existence," that is, to develop *die Fähigkeit der Selbstbewegung*, as he called it. To me, the combination of all these attributes constitutes Guardini's definition of freedom, a freedom without which there can be no genuine knowledge *(Erkenntnis)*.

Concerning the cultured human being: *Mit dem Abstand beginnt die Kultur,* that is, "culture commences with distancing oneself" by refusing to be swept up into the maelstrom of civilization.

Concerning the relationship between religion and literature: Guardini was superbly able to interweave literature, theology and philosophy. This instilled in me a sensitivity to the "awe-fulness" (in the sense of being filled with grandeur and inspired by awe) that is equally present both in sacred texts and in works of great literature.

Second, there were concepts and topics that time and again surfaced throughout the lectures I attended. Interestingly, Guardini had addressed and summarized some of these in a talk he gave on the occasion of the official opening of the Katholische Akademie in Bayern (Catholic Academy of Bavaria) in 1957. The presentation was titled *Kultur als Werk und Gefährdung,* that is, "the task of culture and its dangers." In this talk Guardini reflected on the dual existence of nature, as nature per se and as the sum total of human encounter with it and response to it. To put this another way, Guardini reflected on nature as it presents itself to us *(gegebene)* and also on nature as a task and challenge to us *(aufgegebene)*. He illustrated this dual perception of nature with the example of the

93

great benefits of nuclear energy as well as its inherent lethal and destructive power. Nature is thus both a resource and a danger.

Guardini also spoke of specialization, which hampers the development of the individual person. He observed that scientific, technical and political processes evolve with necessity as well as with a pseudo-religious concept of a fate we cannot escape. As an antidote, he proposed a fourfold cure. First, a vibrant cultural life *(Kulturarbeit)* requires the conscious application of one's talents. Second, for there to be a rich cultural life, there must be a contemplative and meditative center, a genuine inwardness *(Kontemplation)* that is able to ward off the secularizing and distracting tendencies of our age. Third, there is the need for increased self-reliance *(mehr Selbstverantwortung)* and less reliance on the state and neighbor *(weniger Wohlfahrt)*. Fourth, we need to employ the kind of self-discipline *(Askese und Selbstzucht)* that resists reckless consumerism *(Hemmungslosigkeit des Verbrauchens und Genießens)*.

In Guardini's judgment, if we follow these four principles, we will be able to break the stranglehold of inordinate ambition and greed. To this very day, whenever I am about to purchase something less essential, I cannot help but remind myself not to covet the item under consideration. Silly, perhaps, but true. According to Guardini, this kind of self-discipline must not be misconstrued as a denial of life. Rather it must be embraced as a willful affirmation of a freer and more viable life — viable because of its greater degree of value.

For this freedom to exist there must also be, as Guardini insisted, knowledge *(Erkenntnis).* This knowledge or recognition must be understood not as comprehension in quantitative ways; rather, it consists of the ability to discern and act upon opportunities for human growth and dignity.

My third and last recollection is this. With equal vividness, I remember Guardini's concept of *Angerufensein* (sounding through). Guardini would remind his listeners that in the classical Roman theater each performer wore a mask, called a *persona,* through which the performer's voice would be projected, or "sounded through," in a manner similar to speaking through a megaphone. With this image in everyone's mind, Guardini would hammer out the insight that each human being is called by God to develop in relationship to God so that the living God "sounds through" one's personal existence, through the person of each one of us.

In this vein, I am reminded of Guardini's university sermons, which he delivered on Sundays for the academic community that gathered at St. Ludwig Church in Munich. Here Guardini introduced me to Psalm 139, which has been a religious mainstay for me ever since:

O Lord, you have searched me and known me.
You know when I sit down and when I rise up;
   you discern my thoughts from far away.
You search out my path and my lying down,
   and are acquainted with all my ways.
For it was you who formed my inward parts,
   you knit me together in my mother's womb.
I praise you, for I am fearfully and wonderfully made.
   Wonderful are your works; that I know very well.
Search me, O God, and know my heart;
   test me and know my thoughts;
See if there is a wicked way in me,
   and lead me in the way everlasting.
(Psalm 139:1–3, 13–14, 23–24)

In conclusion, I wish to recall Romano Guardini the lecturer, dwarfed by the lectern, in a black suit coat and tie—no Roman collar. Instead he wore what seemed to be an ordinary white shirt. It made him appear less clerical, yet more professorial and academic. If there ever was such a thing as a gentle lecture-hall tyrant, it was Guardini. Pity the person who walked in late; not only was Guardini not distracted, but in fact would turn his head in the direction of the disturbance while continuing to lecture. If the commotion persisted, however—or worse, if he detected students chatting somewhere in the cavernous auditorium—he would briefly interrupt his lecture, eyes flashing, and ask the perpetrators to quiet down or to leave.

One always had the impression that behind the stern reminder was the indignation of a man who knew that he had something to say, that he was going to say it, and that he would be disappointed that there could be someone who had more important things to do in his presence. Why bother to come to his lecture, he seemed to indicate. Clearly, he took himself seriously and, in doing so, also his audience.

III.

The "Sacred Signs" of Romano Guardini

Gertrud Mueller Nelson

I feel I have snuck into this august society on the shirt-tails of those who went before me. My father and mother, the late Dr. Franz Mueller and Dr. Therese Mueller of St. Thomas University (St. Paul, Minnesota), knew Romano Guardini and corresponded with him for many years. There is no doubt that Guardini's spirit breathes in my parents' publications. Also, my godmother, Dr. Gertrud Schuster, was a close friend of Guardini. There's a photograph of her standing with Guardini at Burg Rothenfels. Moreover, over the years my German friends have sent me letters with Germany's commemorative postage stamps of Romano Guardini, which I have prized.

As a matter of fact, I did hear Guardini speak in 1954 at a Sunday student eucharist in Munich's St. Ludwig Church — standing room only. But I was only 17 years old myself. I don't remember what he spoke on; my wobbling household German was being taxed on every front, and I could hardly see him standing in the pulpit from where I stood, in the crush of students much taller than I was at the time. But I remember. And I remember that I was somehow taken up in the power of the moment.

Guardini was a serious and sincere concept to me. My parents spoke of him often. His influence, as I would discover over time by reading his works myself, was considerable in our household. And a book he wrote, *Sacred Signs,* was and still is a favorite of mine. I was given this book on the occasion of my first communion. At the time, I was six-and-a-half years old, as I was fond of reporting, and it was a hot summer day in 1942.

My mother, taken aback by the American way of preparing children for eucharist, had been preparing me — certainly since my birth, but more particularly this hot summer — down in the basement while we were canning tomatoes or peaches or green beans. It was both intense and natural all at once.

Gertrud (G): "How come Jesus wants to hide inside the holy bread?"

Mother (M): "Because everybody knows bread and understands its goodness. We love Jesus and we need Jesus, just as we love bread and we need bread."

G: "How come we can't eat or drink before we receive the holy bread?"

M: "Because we want to feel really hungry — hungry for Jesus."

G: "How come we want to *eat* Jesus?"

M: "Just as you sometimes say you love your baby brother so much you want to eat him — we take Jesus inside us, which is even closer and tighter than a hug."

G: "And if Jesus is in you and me and my sisters and my Oma in Germany and the people in Africa, then Jesus is everywhere! Oh, and then I can't fight with my sisters, because I'd be fighting the Jesus in their hearts! I'd like that very much — Jesus in my heart. I'd like Jesus as my daily bread."

My mother went to the rectory for a talk with Father Moore. She armed herself with courage and, should she need them, the words of a pope: Pius X on early and frequent communion. She explained to Father Moore that I was a somewhat vain child and that if I was required to make my first communion with my class in two years' time I would most certainly get caught up in the froth of the fashion show and minced-step processions. She knew me. Also, she thought I was ready.

Father Moore wasn't so sure. Had I made my first confession? Yes. And if the sisters hadn't yet prepared me for eucharist, who had? My mother pulled herself together and claimed the issue as her holy duty and her privileged right. And what would the other families say? Wouldn't every mother come traipsing in here wanting special privileges? But, she answered, it is their privilege as parents to prepare their children. Furthermore, we Muellers attended Mass at 6:30 each morning. The occasion would be a quiet thing on a weekday — my baptismal day — at the railing between my parents and with my sisters. Well (said Father Moore), I needed examination.

And so it was that I took my mother's hand and we went again to the rectory. The heat and humidity were oppressive. My fear of Father Moore was the same terror that every kid in the school had. He had trouble hearing, and if you went to his stall for confession, he'd yell at you if you didn't speak up. He'd repeat your sins for the world to hear — just to make sure he got them right! His stiff leg always protruded from under the confessional door, certainly an outward sign of his propensity to "trip one up."

I sat on a hard chair in the rectory's sitting room, waiting for my interrogator to enter. The shades were drawn against the burning sun, and I felt a trickle of sweat streak down my face. It's odd, the details one remembers! Father Moore came in and sat down across his desk from me. "Your name?" he bellowed; "What did I want?" I wanted Jesus to come into my heart. "Oh, yes."

I was to explain the meaning of "holy communion." I was to prove that I knew what to do with my teeth and tongue. I was to make the sign of the cross and recite an Our Father, a Hail Mary and a Glory Be. I was to recite the Act of Contrition. I don't remember the other questions, save one: "What does it mean to amend your life?" "Mend," I said promptly. "It means to mend. Like patching a sock. You make a sin and you have to darn the hole and make it right again." I passed.

On my first communion day, my mother took my linen baptismal robe, with my name and symbols of all seven sacraments embroidered on it, and wrapped it around my waist and secured it. Then she pulled my Sunday dress over the top of it. No one else would know it was there, the white dress of my baptism that would go with me to the altar railing, my baptismal robe that would be pinned up again years later under my wedding dress. I had a huge, tall baptismal candle which was left burning for me at home, and the family walked up the hill to the church. It was on this occasion that my parents gave me a gift, *Sacred Signs*—a worn book that I still have and re-read on occasion. Not the plastic-coated prayer book of my peers, but a grown-up's book: *Sacred Signs.* I could read it all by myself. I could understand it! I could use it. And best of all, I never had to outgrow it.

IV.

Romano Guardini's *Akademische Feier* in 1964

Thomas F. O'Meara, OP

In the summer of 1963, my Dominican superiors decided to send me to Munich, Germany, to do a doctorate in theology. Up until that time almost all American Dominicans received their graduate education either in Rome or in Fribourg, Switzerland. But because of ecumenism and the emergence of contemporary theology with Vatican II, it was necessary for my province to have some members who knew something about philosophy and theology after 1600.

I arrived in Munich on a rainy Sunday evening in October, 1963, and a month later, as the winter semester began, I attended my first lectures at Ludwig-Maximilian University.

A year had passed when in February, 1965, I was walking down the streets near the university and noticed on one of the kiosks a placard, like those listing the many concerts and lectures in the Bavarian capital, which said that there would be an *Akademische Feier,* an academic celebration, in honor of Romano Guardini's 80th birthday. Like most Americans of my generation, I knew him only through the book *The Lord* and through a few articles in *Worship* or *Jubilee* that mentioned him. *The Lord* was handsomely printed, and its jacket was adorned with a painting by Rouault, a sign of a tentative acquaintance with modernity. I doubt that I knew Guardini was from an Italian family that had lived for three decades in Germany. I had been surprised to learn not long after my arrival that Guardini was at Munich. I did not know his serious works on modern philosophy and literature.

On February 17, I made a point of going to the Aula Maxima on the first floor of the Main Building of the *"Uni."* The crowd was dense, and one could not get far into the balcony area. The first floor was reserved for dignitaries invited to this *Hochansehnliche Festversammlung* ("Highly Reputable Festival Gathering"). When I gave up and came down to the main floor, the assembly was ending. I caught a glimpse of a frail figure leaving the auditorium and being congratulated. He was more fragile and thin and rather shorter than I had expected. It was the famous Romano Guardini; nearby was Karl Rahner.

The opening remarks of the celebration were by Hans Wolfgang Müller, dean of the faculty of philosophy. He touched on the war years, on Guardini's struggle in Berlin against the violence of 1929–1939, and on his removal from that University. After the war, teaching in Tübingen, he had helped restore German university life. Coming to Munich in 1948, he had been a major interpreter for Germans—young and old, Catholics and agnostics—of the course of modernity. Müller said:

> The faculty owe you, most respected jubilarian, a most respectful debt of gratitude for an activity rich in blessings and blessed in riches, an activity undertaken in silence and in a broad public arena, an activity deeply marked by a personal tone, something seldom found in a professor. In our time of need immediately after the total collapse [of Nazi Germany], concerned to give to the youth returning to our university from chaos the right teacher for the themes of humanity and of reflection on the basic foundations of our existence, the dean of our philosophy faculty at that time, Alexander Sharff, extended to you in September 1945 an invitation to take on this challenge. Three years later . . . you accepted the call to our faculty. During the next fifteen years in your teaching here in Munich you gathered around yourself a large community in the biggest auditorium at our university. You, a theologian,

have developed philosophically in your lectures your content of faith and interacted in the realms of the history of ideas with the religious questions of the present and the past. . . . From the heritage of antiquity, the Church Fathers, and the great works of literature, from Plato, Augustine, Dante, Pascal, Hölderlin, Dostoevski and Rilke you let appear the image of human existence, the eternal order of the world, the essence of the divine. . . . Through your unusual personality and wisdom you overcame the problems of the unconventional academic chair for Christian worldview and the philosophy of religion within a philosophical faculty. You yourself have given to your own academic field an innovative approach. In a gifted way you have spoken to young people and drawn them into your interests. This attraction has its source in the natural authority which comes from your personality and from your wisdom concerning divine matters.[5]

After this address, Helmut Kuhn, a professor whose lectures and writings also treated the broad area of Catholicism and culture, presented Guardini with a large *Festschrift.* This honorary volume, which Germans often publish to commemorate the anniversaries of academics, was filled with contributions by professors (other professors had often ignored him as an outsider in nationality and in scientific rigor) and congratulations by bishops (few had supported him during his creative explorations of modern philosophy and literature). Among those contributing to this 750-page volume were Paul Ricoeur, Gabriel Marcel, Friedrich Heiler, Hans Urs von Balthasar, Heinrich Fries, J. B. Lotz and Karl Rahner.[6]

Inside the *aula,* the modest but energetic figure of Karl Rahner had given the main address, the *Festvortrag.* He was Guardini's successor in the interdisciplinary professorship whose field was titled Philosophy of Religion and Christian Worldview. He had taken up his professorial responsibilities in March of 1964 with lectures on the foundations of Christian faith, a theology that he later published as his mature system. Guardini's life, Rahner began, is a long and rich one, and his work is extensive. Life and work form a totality, and today in this celebration both are being celebrated.

We are near St. Ludwig Church. It prompts us to recall Guardini the preacher, the academic preacher who can speak to all, the preacher without external pathos. He does not command when he preaches; he does not instruct; he does not distribute condescendingly from the pulpit self-secure warnings about orthodoxy. He draws the hearer into his own questions . . . and he lets the word of God in the scripture be personally taken into one's life.[7]

Rahner ended by talking about the forces at work in Guardini's era and about the priest's influence upon young people in the years after the First World War. He mentioned Max Scheler's advice to Guardini. The phenomenologist told him not to give lectures on the philosophy of religion but to unveil great thinkers and great books, to reveal the poetry and painting of Dante and Rembrandt. In Rahner's words:

> In these interpretations Guardini brought his thinking through differentiation and assimilation to meet a large part of the tradition of the Western spirit. But he saw himself working at "the end of the modern age," in a time of transition, at the edge of a barren and hard time without any Muses. Still, the past would remain vital, unburdening itself of its contributions for our future.[8]

Guardini's response was not audible at the rear of the balcony where I had been standing. Eighty years of age, he had been ill for some time and would live less than three more years. He died in 1968 and is buried in Munich. I learned later that this remarkably personal teacher, at such a climactic and emotional moment, had chosen to speak of Plato and of the young Glaucon, whose words introduced the theme of the role of uncertainty, irony and skepticism in the unfolding of truth. Truth — he alluded to the Augustinian Bonaventure, on whom he had written his dissertation years before — is not a rational simplicity but an *excessivum*. The situation of the knowing person is characterized by experiencing. There is certainly absolute truth, but that is God. The human person never adequately realizes that kind of truth. "Human beings betray humanity's nobility when they understand their world from below; they live correctly when they live from above down."[9]

Authorities say that Pope Paul VI, at the time of this birthday celebration, offered Guardini a cardinal's hat, but that the elderly priest refused it. Earlier, when he was young, ecclesiastical honors would have had some meaning. But Vatican officials and his own diocese ignored him from 1919 to 1953, arguably the most important years of his theological scholarship and pastoral leadership.

One last recollection, indirect but quite personal: Curiously and paradoxically, Guardini's chair and his retirement caused me some difficulty. That academic position, as I mentioned, was in the department of philosophy. Rahner, in accepting that chair and by coming to Munich from Innsbruck, certainly had an understanding, probably explicit but at least implicit, that he would be able to direct doctoral students in the faculty of theology. Rahner was very clearly a theologian: His lectures and seminars at Munich, and his publications and his work at Vatican II then taking place in Rome, were theological. I was aspiring to be one of his students.

But when he arrived, he learned that he could direct doctoral students only in philosophy. I heard rumors of this situation, and by late summer 1964 it had become clear that this injustice was occurring. There was considerable envy of Rahner among some, though not all, of the theology professors. Already famous in Germany, his international reputation and the important role he would play in Catholic life in the conciliar

Romano Guardini
in Mooshausen,
August 1965.

era was evident. So I had to find another *Doktor-Vater*. Fortunately, Heinrich Fries, who was the ordinary professor for the area that interested me, fundamental theology, worked together with Rahner on projects and respected his theology. I could go to him and find a friendly reception. Three years later Karl Rahner moved to the University of Münster.[10]

Romano Guardini and Karl Rahner: two great figures in German Catholicism's dialogue with modernity. Guardini's sermons and books were preliminary studies for Vatican II. They were an inspiration for theologians and pastors who would work for and enact the ideals of the Council, and for younger theologians, bishops and laity who were already in 1965 imagining a church transcending European culture — Rahner's "world church." Guardini gave Catholics permission to enter the *Neuzeit,* the "new age," a term that was in the titles of dozens of books in the 1930s and again in the 1960s. Even as he transcended this new age's dangers, he led, courageously and at times alone, into the stages during this century in which Catholics gained an understanding of the self, existence, cultural history, the reality and intelligibility of atheism and the splendor of liturgy well done. He wrote of his own work:

> It became clear to me what Christian worldview is: the perduring, that is the methodical encounter between faith and the world, not just the world in general but in concrete, in culture and its forms, in history, in social life. So my books . . . are not literary criticism nor theology but are meetings, a look from one to the other.[11]

Guardini and Rahner understood that Catholicism could not forever hide from the modern world in the labyrinth of neo-scholasticism. Both knew modern thought well enough not to be frightened of it. Each represented the open, creative milieu of German Catholic intellectuals after World War I, a dynamic intellectual life which had its roots in the nineteenth century.[12] Guardini was older and so preparatory, less focused on precise theological topics, the topics whose historical forms Rahner explored so brilliantly. Rahner was in the line of Aquinas, while Guardini drew inspiration and insight from Bonaventure. Rahner's thought is a kind of heightened, modern exposition of Aquinas's theology of primal Truth, the Holy Spirit, and grace as formal cause; Guardini emphasizes the dynamics of love and longing seeking the divine Friend. Like Guardini, Rahner, too, could write prayers, sermons and poetry, but his theology remained within the boundaries of an existential and historical metaphysics; Guardini's soared outward toward what mysticism, worship and art revere.

Endnotes

1. See Regina Kuehn, *A Place for Baptism* (Chicago: Liturgy Training Publications, 1992), 130 ff.

2. See Regina Kuehn, "Romano Guardini: The Teacher of Teachers," in Robert L. Tuzik (ed.), *How Firm A Foundation: Leaders of the Liturgical Movement* (Chicago: Liturgy Training Publications, 1990), 36 – 49, 36.

3. Editor's note: At the Guardini Conference itself, here followed a slide presentation concerning Guardini's life at Mooshausen from the summer of 1943 until the autumn of 1945.

4. This gratitude motivated my recent translation: Hans Urs von Balthasar, *Romano Guardini,* trans. Albert K. Wimmer (San Francisco: Ignatius Press, forthcoming).

5. Hans W. Müller, "Grusswort," in Karl Foster (ed.), *Akademische Feier zum 80. Geburtstag von Romano Guardini* (Würzburg: Echter Verlag, 1965), 10 – 11. Editor's note: Throughout this fourth reminiscence the translations from the original German texts are by T. O'Meara.

6. Helmut Kuhn, Heinrich Kahlefeld, Karl Forster (eds.), *Interpretation der Welt* (Würzburg: Echter Verlag, 1965).

7. Karl Rahner, "Festvortrag," in Forster, 17 – 35, 22.

8. Ibid., 23.

9. Romano Guardini, "Wahrheit und Ironie," in Forster, 36 – 41.

10. See Karl Rahner, *I Remember,* trans. Harvey D. Egan (New York: Crossroad, 1985), 73 – 75.

11. Romano Guardini, *Stationen und Rückblicke* (Würzburg: Echter, 1965), 9.

12. See Thomas F. O'Meara, *Church and Culture: German Catholic Theology, 1860 – 1914* (Notre Dame: University of Notre Dame Press, 1991).

Chapter Eight

Romano Guardini's Spirit Today: A Meditation

Gertrud Mueller Nelson

I t seems interesting to me that in the course of my growing up, some of the mentors I tracked were echoes and affirmations of what I was learning through the pores of my skin from Romano Guardini: Virgil Michel, Gerald Vann, Thomas Merton, Carl Jung, Maria Montessori. Certainly they were contemporaries. I wonder sometimes if Guardini and Montessori ever crossed paths. Guardini mentioned Montessori in his introduction to *Sacred Signs*. And though I can't attest to it, one senses the mark of Guardini's sensibilities for ritual and symbol and for reverence for the ordinary stuff of a well-rooted life in Montessori's pedagogy: in what she calls the "Exercises of Practical Life," her education of the senses, and in her liturgically oriented approach to religious education.

Carl Jung was known to have told a gathering of Anglican bishops in the early 1930s that they subjected religious mystery too much to their playful intellects. He urged them to lay off trying to understand every dogma and begin simply to immerse themselves in holy action and sacramental gesture. Our intellect, he said, does not understand the secrets of religious mystery. He said that Roman Catholic liturgy, its feasts and seasons, its sacraments and sacramentals — if one really *lived* the rhythm of this cycle — had everything necessary to becoming whole, healed and holy. Jung's enormous recognition in the churches — even if vigorously shunned in academia — tells of a growing sensibility for the symbolic life.

Then I discovered Gerald Vann — and more recently, that he quoted D. H. Lawrence. Said Vann:

> Few of us nowadays can be countrymen, can have the countryman's nearness to the earth or his deep knowledge and love of it; for most of us life means city life, and it is easy for us to become remote from the realities of nature and its yearly rhythm, easy to

become uprooted from our mother earth. Yet to allow this to happen is to invite disaster; a deep sickness of mind and heart; and that is why not only Christians but non-Christians too have sensed the church's wisdom in keeping us close to that yearly rhythm through its liturgical cycle. It was not a Catholic, it was D. H. Lawrence who, lamenting the fact that so many of us nowadays "are bleeding at the roots because we are cut off from the earth and sun and stars," remarked how Catholicism had on the contrary preserved for us "the rhythm of life itself . . . day by day, season by season, year by year" and how that coming of the seasons and going of the seasons is the "inward rhythm of man and woman, too, the sadness of Lent, the delight of Easter, the wonder of Pentecost."[1]

D. H. Lawrence, to be sure, was no liturgist. But he held the same apprehension of the liturgist, namely, that we are doomed when we lose touch with cycles of nature and a simple life, because we will then lose touch with our own seasons of dying and rising, of growing and becoming.

Gerald Vann was attentive to Jung and liturgy early on — his theology was decidedly incarnational, and like Guardini he never found much recognition or respect in the official church before Vatican II. And who remembers him now? But he always taught the holiness of matter and linked the cycles of Christ's life to the rhythms of our own in ways I found human and sustaining.

Virgil Michel said, "Just live the liturgy . . . and you will realize the need of sharing in Christ's Calvaries to have a share also in his resurrections." In this vein, Romano Guardini observed that with the birth of the modern world, we lost contact with the basic elements of life, with the natural order. As a result, we also suffered the loss of connectedness with the divine order. Only by reknitting our ties with the earth can we hope to revive our awareness of God and renew our worship. In Guardini's words:

> The liturgy is not merely thought, nor is it merely emotion; it is first and foremost development, growth, ripening, being. The liturgy is a process of fulfillment, a growth to maturity. The whole of nature must be evoked by the liturgy, and as the liturgy seized by grace must take hold of it all, refine and glorify it in the likeness of Christ, through the all-embracing and ardent love of the Holy Ghost for the glory of the Father, whose sovereign Majesty draws all things to Itself. Thus the liturgy embraces everything in existence, angels, men [and women] and things; all the content and events of life; in short, the whole of reality.[2]

About Seeing and Doing

So it was that Guardini reminded us that the way to a liturgical life does not go through mere teaching, but before all else goes through doing. Seeing and doing are the groundwork on which all the rest is founded — doing, and a true doing, not a mere practicing. Doing is elementary, and it employs the whole of us and all our creative powers. It is alive; it is an experience; it is an undertaking; it is seeing.

And are we not, in a moment of seeing and recognition, in turn, seen and recognized, called and named?

Moses

I wonder if one of the early stories in the Hebrew scriptures about Moses is not a story about a liturgy of seeing and doing: Moses is wandering about in the desert, herding his father-in-law's sheep (Exodus 3).[3]

What could be more boring? We know this place! Perhaps it is when we find ourselves stuck in traffic, or feeling routinized in our daily rounds, overwhelmed by a gray world. We despair of anything so glorious as a religious experience as we drive the kids to the dentist or pay our bills. What landscape could be less interesting? There is nothing to look forward to — nothing on this bleak horizon. Well, maybe there's a bush. Or is it a fire?

Like Moses, we could regard this occurrence as merely a bush or merely a fire and then trod on in our boring lives. But at the moment Moses sees the bush, he stops what he is doing and turns aside for a moment from his outer purpose of herding sheep. He looks, and then he sees: This is a bush on fire, and what's more, the bush is not burning up.

So Moses allows and accepts the great paradox of opposites in this phenomenon. By superimposing and holding the tension of two opposing factors, his vision pierces through the ordinary world of appearances. The ordinary bush and the Spirit-fire become one and the same thing. Moses is attentive to what he sees; he *names* the revelation and makes it conscious. He approaches the holy ground. And in approaching, *he* is called and named: Moses, Moses! And Moses answers: Here I am.

No reply could be more ordinary — or more profound. Only in our ordinariness can we stand simply before God. And, with an ordinary gesture, we remove our shoes that we might be even more grounded and in contact with the ground of our being. Earthed. Rooted. In touch. Planted firmly in this, the present moment. This is indeed

Holy Ground. Here I am. For which awareness we are given an experience of God. We hear God's name: not "Here I am this time," but even more simply, "I AM."

With that mutual naming, Moses has an identity. He is given a vocation, and meaning is returned to his life. He is changed — transformed! But, of course, he still lisps, he still feels like a misfit. He doubts that his ordinariness will allow him to win friends or influence people — much less impress the people he is to lead to freedom. Hardly has he been moved to the very core of his being that he doubts he has the necessary qualifications — and he wants to argue about it! Even as he gets an identity, he has an identity crisis! And yet, Moses is sent forward to do God's work. He becomes a prophet and a liberator of his people.

Elements of Rite

What are the elements of rite? Stopping. "Seeing and doing," as Guardini pointed out. Listening and going forth. Stop. Look. Listen. Do and go forth.

Stop

First one must stop. Whenever life loses meaning or becomes routinized, we must stop. Milling around causes us to lose meaning and purpose. We lose faith. We forget what we are about. Life looks like a desert even as we stand at the mountain of the Lord. Life is so much herding of sheep. Or worse, we may not even have the natural entities of dumb creatures to care for but are caught in mindless work or the manipulation of inanimate things.

So stopping promptly allows us to "take time." To take time is not to waste time, spend time or kill time. It is time taken out of the routine context and set apart: time out of time, which is the nature of Sunday and the rhythm of the feast. Time taken and dedicated draws a sacred circle around a moment — marks that moment, sets it aside and focuses us.

The action of liturgy begins with a new twist: Don't just do something! Stand there! Holding still allows our vision and our action to become inspired. In a hurried world, standing still is seen as impractical. And isn't the practical so often the enemy of the holy?

Look

Having now stopped, we can look. We focus. And thus we will see that the everyday and the sacred, the ordinary and the extraordinary, can meet. Essentially, we allow what is split in us and divides us from the sacred and our very selves to re-unite and become one, holy, and universal.

It helps to remember that we cannot find the holy outside the ordinary stuff of our daily lives and our human experiences. The flesh-taking of the spirit, the incarnation, is made new in our daily efforts to wed heaven and earth. For Moses, the ordinary bush and the spirit-fire join, become a single entity and, what is more, do not cancel each other out but now bless and enhance each other!

In eucharist, the ordinary bread and the person of Christ become a single entity through the spirit. In looking, we will "see the world in a grain of sand." We experience "eternity in an hour." Every material thing and every human relationship will be shot through and shining with grace. Now we are truly human.

The scholar
in his 70s.

Do

Thus, we are moved to do something! We approach, but we take off our shoes. An experience of God is more likely to come to us from the bottom up than from the top down. The kingdom of God is at hand. In fact, the kingdom of God is underfoot, if we can approach with barefoot vulnerability. Rarely, as we have already said, does an experience of God take place outside the ordinary, earthy elements of our existence.

Just so must the creative and poetic church return to us with meaning and right worth (*worship* means worth-ship), the simplest elements of this material world as infused with grace and redeemed. "Look, here God lives among human beings. He will make his home among them; they will be his people, and he will be their God. God-with-us." For the kingdom of God is not so much a place as it is an experience. It is God's saving power made manifest.

The kingdom is astonishingly at hand and familiar: indeed, in bread and wine, in fire and ash, in oil and water, in darkness and light, in the sacrificed sweet odor of incense and the ancient words of the sacred story, in gesture and action, in songs and sounds and sacred silence. Through the very pores of our skins, through the soles of our bare feet, we draw up the sacred into our humanity. Thus, Christian ritual will always draw its action from what is most human in us, more than from heady ideas in theology. We do something.

We take off our shoes. We break the bread. We drink the cup. We tell the story. For signs and symbols are the earthy foundation of liturgy. We retrieve what has been lost, that which is essential to proper performance of prayer in liturgy: gesture. Romano Guardini said:

> In olden times people knew that outward bearing and behavior were not superficial things. They become superficial only when they have lost their inner meaning. Gesture reaches from the hand back to the heart. Outward bearing is rooted in inner attitude. It expresses what lives within; what the heart feels and the mind intends. Conversely it can itself affect the inner life, giving it stability and form.[4]

Listen

Barefoot and firmly planted, we now listen. For we will be called and named. In baptism we have been named and chosen. And, in hearing the call, we will know what we must be about. We will have an identity infused with grace. We will always be nothing more than the most ordinary human being — inept, lisping, broken, faltering, making excuses — and thus infinitely suited to becoming a prophet among the people.

Go Forth

And so it is that liturgy always calls us to action and returns us to the community with a vocation there to love and serve the Lord and to live simply, in what Guardini refers to as a "progressive return." Humankind, said Guardini in 1930,

> has fallen away on the one hand into a world of abstraction, on the other into the purely physical sphere; from union with nature into the purely scholastic and artificial; from the community into isolation. Our deepest longing should be to become once more one of the people; not indeed by romantic attempts to conform with popular ideas and customs, but by a renewal of our inmost spirit by a *progressive return* to a simple and complete life.[5]

A progressive return will send us forth "to love and serve the Lord" in the community. It means not just to be consumers of the gospel but to give flesh to it. I am always struck at how far afield we have drifted since the liturgical prophets pointed out how the communal action of liturgy always sends us forward into responsibility for the community.

How many a parish council these days has one committee for liturgy and another for social justice, and the two never affect or even talk to each other? The liturgists busy themselves with swathing the church with bolts of gold lamé for Christmas, and the social justice crowd is writing postcards to their senator. Neither is necessarily wrong, but the former action is in danger of being reduced to glitzy stage-prop design, and the latter action may be disconnected from an organic connection to sacred worship. Rosemary Haughton says that Christians need to recover an earthy spirituality "if the Church is to be prophetic, wild and holy, and not merely socially enlightened."[6]

Liturgy always calls us to action and returns us to the community with a vocation there to love and serve the Lord and to live simply, in what Guardini refers to as a "progressive return."

Liturgy is not the religion of an elite, nor of the elite ritual artist or the politically enlightened. Rather it is the religion of the people because it cuts beyond abstract ideas and is simply up and doing what the human heart already knows. And liturgy returns us to community because if the saving power of God is to be manifest in each of us — in the graced reality of our lives — and in the stuff of this earth, then our concerns must become communal, ecological, global. Liturgy is inclusive because in the realm of being and gesture, images and rites, there is a form for the practical and the profound, the hero and the mystic, and the direct and earthy experience of mystery.

Finally, it was individualism that Guardini saw as the dangerous result of our being cut off from nature. And indeed, individualism and self-centeredness are the hallmarks of the contemporary American. A celebration of eucharist should enable the individual to act with a visceral commitment to the cause of justice and liberation. The liturgical prayer of the community leads us to the mission of the church in the world. It reorients us to our vocation as priestly workers among the people. As it used to be said, God became man that man might become God: God took on our humanity so that we as ordinary and human could do the extraordinary work of God.

And when, as a people of God, we find ourselves lost in a swirling morass of "shoulds" and "oughts," disjointed, alienated from nature, one another, God and even ourselves, at this moment there is a gesture, profoundly at hand, that will draw us up and put us together. Recall what Guardini wrote in his little book *Sacred Signs.* In his

111

very first essay, he speaks of that gesture — the sign of the cross. There are those who might call it pure Zen:

> When we cross ourselves, let it be with a real sign of the cross. Instead of a small cramped gesture that gives no notion of its meaning, let us make a large unhurried sign, from forehead to breast, from shoulder to shoulder, consciously feeling how it includes the whole of us, our thoughts, our attitudes, our body and soul, every part of us at once, how it consecrates and sanctifies us.
>
> It does so because it is the sign of the universe and the sign of our redemption. On the cross Christ redeemed [hu]mankind. By the cross he sanctifies [us] to the last shred and fibre of [our] being. We make the sign of the cross before we pray to collect and compose ourselves and to fix our minds and hearts and wills upon God. We make it when we finish praying in order that we may hold fast the gift we have received from God. In temptations we sign ourselves to be strengthened; in dangers, to be protected. The cross is signed upon us in blessings in order that the fullness of God's life may flow into the soul and fructify and sanctify us wholly.
>
> Think of these things when you make the sign of the cross. It is the holiest of all signs. Make a large cross, taking time, thinking what you do. Let it take in your whole being — body, soul, mind, will, thoughts, feelings, your doing and not-doing — and by signing it with the cross strengthen and consecrate the whole in the strength of Christ, in the name of the triune God.[7]

Let us end our reflection on Guardini's spirit with the sign of the cross: In the name of the Father, and of the Son and of the Holy Spirit. Amen.

Endnotes

1. Gerald Vann, *The Son's Course* (London: Fontana, 1958), 10. Vann is quoting D. H. Lawrence's *Apropos of Lady Chatterley's Lover.*

2. Romano Guardini, *The Church and the Catholic,* trans. Ada Lane (New York: Sheed and Ward, 1935), 29 – 30.

3. Editor's note: This meditation on Exodus 3 is a variation on the reflection shared in Gertrud Mueller Nelson, *To Dance with God* (Mahwah: Paulist Press, 1986), 17. This book itself manifests the spirit of Romano Guardini.

4. Romano Guardini, *Prayer in Practice,* trans. Prince Leopold of Loewenstein-Wertheim (New York: Pantheon, 1957), 38 – 39.

5. Guardini, *The Church and the Catholic,* 20.

6. Rosemary Haughton is quoted in Margaret Quigley and Michael Garvey (eds.), *Dorothy Day Book* (Springfield, Illinois: Templegate, 1982), 110.

7. Romano Guardini, *Sacred Signs,* trans. Grace Branham (St. Louis: Pio Decimo, 1956), 13–14.

Robert A. Krieg, CSC

I. Books in English by Romano Guardini, including the date of the original German text (G)

The Art of Praying. Trans. Prince Leopold of Loewenstein-Wertheim. Mansfield, New Hampshire: Sophia Institute Press, 1994. Formerly: *Prayer in Practice,* 1957. G: 1943.

The Church of the Lord. Trans. Stella Lange. Chicago: Henry Regnery, 1966. G: 1965.

The Church and the Catholic. Trans. Ada Lane. New York: Sheed and Ward, 1935. G: 1922.

The Death of Socrates. Trans. Basil Wrighton. New York: Sheed and Ward, 1948. G: 1943.

The End of the Modern World. Trans. Joseph Theman and Herbert Burke. New York: Sheed and Ward, 1956. G: 1950.

Faith and the Modern Man. Trans. Charlotte E. Forsyth. New York: Pantheon Books, 1952. G: 1944.

Freedom, Grace and Destiny. Trans. John Murray. New York: Pantheon Books, 1961. G: 1948.

The Humanity of Christ. Trans. Ronald Walls. New York: Pantheon Books, 1964. G: 1958.

Jesus Christus: Meditations. Trans. Peter White. Chicago: Henry Regnery, 1959. G: 1957.

Letters from Lake Como. Trans. Geoffrey W. Bromiley. Grand Rapids: William B. Eerdmans, 1994. G: 1927.

The Life of Faith. Trans. John Chapin. Westminster, Maryland: Newman, 1961. G: 1935.

The Living God. Trans. Stanley Godman. New York: Pantheon Books, 1957. G: 1929.

The Lord. Trans. Elinor Castendyk Briefs. Chicago: Henry Regnery, 1954. G: 1937.

The Lord's Prayer. Trans. Isabel McHugh. New York: Pantheon Books, 1958. G: 1932.

Meditations Before Mass. Trans. Elinor Castendyk Briefs. Westminster, Maryland: Newman, 1955. Reprinted: Mansfield, New Hampshire: Sophia Institute Press, 1993. G: 1939.

Pascal for Our Time. Trans. Brian Thompson. New York: Herder and Herder, 1966. G: 1935.

Power and Responsibility. Trans. Elinor C. Briefs. Chicago: Henry Regnery, 1961. G: 1951.

Prayer in Practice. Trans. Prince Leopold Loewenstein-Wertheim, 1963. Reprinted as *The Art of Praying,* 1994. G: 1943.

Prayers From Theology. Trans. Richard Newnham. New York: Herder and Herder, 1956. G: 1948.

Rilke's Duino Elegies. Trans. K. G. Knight. Chicago: Henry Regnery, 1961. G: 1953.

The Rosary of Our Lady. Trans. H. von Schuecking. New York: Kenedy, 1955. Reprinted: Mansfield, New Hampshire: Sophia Institute Press, 1994. G: 1940.

Sacred Signs. Trans. Grace Branham. St. Louis: Pio Decimo, 1956. G: 1929.

The Spirit of the Liturgy. Trans. Ada Lane. New York: Sheed and Ward, 1935. G: 1918.

The Virtues. Trans. Stella Lange. Chicago: Henry Regnery, 1967. G: 1963.

The Wisdom of the Psalms. Trans. Stella Lange. Chicago: Henry Regnery, 1968. G: 1963.

The World and the Person. Trans. Stella Lange. Chicago: Henry Regnery, 1965. G: 1939.

The Word of God on Faith, Hope and Charity. Trans. Stella Lange. Chicago: Henry Regnery, 1963. G: 1949.

II. Publications in English on Romano Guardini

"Candid Monsignor." *Newsweek* 45 (10 January 1955): 50.

"Death of Romano Guardini." *Tablet* 222 (12 October 1968): 1021.

"Faith is the Center." *Time* 75 (14 March 1960): 51.

Balthasar, Hans Urs von. *Romano Guardini.* Translated by Albert Wimmer. San Francisco: Ignatius Press, forthcoming.

Berger, Teresa. "The Classical Liturgical Movement in Germany and Austria: Moved by Women?" *Worship* 66 (May 1992): 231–50.

Borghesi, Massimo. "Reflection: A New Beginning." *30 Days* 5 (1992): 62–68.

Farrugia, Mario. "Romano Guardini (1885–1968)." In René Latourelle and Rino Fisichella (eds.), *Dictionary of Fundamental Theology,* 403–406. New York: Crossroad, 1995.

Hill, Roland. "Spiritual Liberator." *The Catholic World Report* 1 (June 1992): 52–55.

Krieg, Robert A. "Romano Guardini: Forerunner of Vatican II." *America* 169 (5 February 1993): 24–25.

_____ . "Romano Guardini: Paving the Way for Vatican II." *National Catholic Register* 70 (24 July 1994): 1, 9.

Kuehn, Regina. "Romano Guardini: Teacher of Teachers." In *How Firm A Foundation: Leaders of the Liturgical Movement,* edited by Robert Tuzik, 36–49. Chicago: Liturgy Training Publications, 1990.

Laubach, Jakob. "Romano Guardini." In *Theologians of Our Time,* edited by Leonhard Reinisch and translated by Charles H. Henkey, 109–26. Notre Dame: University of Notre Dame Press, 1964. The original German text appeared in 1960.

Misner, Paul. "Guardini, Romano." In *New Catholic Encyclopedia,* 16: *Supplement 1967–1974,* edited by David Eggenberger, 198–99. Washington, D.C.: Publishers Guild, Inc. with McGraw-Hill Book Company, 1974.

Rahner, Karl. "Romano Guardini's Successor." In K. Rahner, *I Remember,* translated by Harvey D. Egan, 73–75. New York: Crossroad, 1985.

_____ . "Thinker and Christian: Obituary of Romano Guardini." In K. Rahner, *Opportunities for Faith,* translated by Edward Quinn, 127–31. New York: The Seabury Press, 1975. The original German text appeared in 1968.

Schoof, T. Mark. *A Survey of Catholic Theology 1800–1970.* Translated by N. D. Smith, 81–84, passim. New York: Paulist Newman Press, 1970.

Contributors

LAWRENCE S. CUNNINGHAM, professor and chairman of the Department of Theology at the University of Notre Dame, is the author of 16 books and more than 125 articles on the Catholic faith and the spiritual life. His books include *Catholic Prayer* (1989), *Thomas Merton* (1992) and *Culture and Values* (3rd Edition, 1993).

KATHLEEN HUGHES, RSCJ, is professor of liturgy at Catholic Theological Union, Chicago. She is the editor of *How Firm a Foundation: Voices of the Early Liturgical Movement* (1990), and author of *The Monk's Tale: A Biography of Godfrey Diekmann* (1991) and numerous articles on worship and church life. She recently received a major grant from the Lilly Foundation to study Sunday worship in Catholic parishes without priests.

ROBERT A. KRIEG, CSC, is associate professor in the Department of Theology, at the University of Notre Dame. He is the author of *Story-Shaped Christology* (1988), *Karl Adam* (1992) and articles on modern German christology.

HEINZ R. KUEHN of Oak Park, Illinois, is an independent scholar who grew up in Germany during the Nazi era. A convert to Catholicism and a member of the organized resistance movement, he participated in Guardini's circles in Berlin and Tübingen. After emigrating to America in 1951, he specialized in medical writing and publishing. Both in Germany and the United States he has published numerous essays on religious, literary and philosophical subjects. He is also the author of several books, including an autobiographical memoir, *Mixed Blessings: An Almost Ordinary Life in Hitler's Germany* (1989).

REGINA KUEHN of Oak Park, Illinois, is an artist and liturgical theologian who grew up in Germany during the Nazi era. At the University of Berlin, she was closely associated with Romano Guardini and wrote her doctoral dissertation under his direction. Today she serves as a consultant for liturgical art and architecture in the archdiocese of Chicago. Her writings include "Romano Guardini" in *How Firm a Foundation: Leaders of the Liturgical Movement* (1990) and *A Place for Baptism* (1992).

GERTRUD MUELLER NELSON of Del Mar, California, is an artist, writer and lecturer. Born in Cologne, Germany, her parents were friends of Romano Guardini. Her formal study includes Montessori education, print-making in Germany and work at the Carl Jung Institute in Zurich. She has written *To Dance with God* (1986) and *Here All Dwell Free* (1991), has published two books of liturgical art and has written articles for religious and catechetical journals.

THOMAS F. O'MEARA, OP, is the William K. Warren Professor of Theology at the University of Notre Dame. Past president of the Catholic Theological Society of America and the North American Paul Tillich Society, he is the author of many books and articles. Among his most recent books are *Theology of Ministry* (1983), *Romantic Idealism and Roman Catholicism* (1982) and *Church and Culture: German Catholic Theology, 1860–1914* (1991).

ARNO SCHILSON is Professor of Western Religions at the University of Mainz, Germany. His books include *Christologie im Präsens* (1980), co-authored with Bishop Walter Kasper, and *Perspektiven Theologischer Erneuerung* (1986), which presents the theology of Romano Guardini. As the theological consultant to Burg Rothenfels am Main, he leads two scholarly symposia each year on Guardini's life and thought. He is also the president of the International Lessing Society.

ALBERT K. WIMMER, who was born in Germany, is associate professor in the Department of German/Russian Language and Literature at the University of Notre Dame. At the University of Munich, he took courses with Romano Guardini. Author of *The Anthology of Medieval German Literature* (1987, 1991), he has recently finished an English translation of Hans Urs von Balthasar's *Romano Guardini* (1970), which will be published by Ignatius Press.

Other Resources on the History of the Liturgical Movement Available from Liturgy Training Publications

The First Fifty Years, video. A series of interviews with leaders of the liturgical movement who gathered in 1990 to celebrate the 50th anniversary of the Liturgical Weeks that began in Chicago in 1940.

How Firm a Foundation: Voices of the Early Liturgical Movement. Compiled and introduced by Kathleen Hughes, RSCJ. Short quotes from the writings and talks of the early leaders of the liturgical movement.

How Firm a Foundation: Leaders of the Liturgical Movement. Compiled by Robert Tuzik. A book on the lives and work of more than 40 pioneers and recent leaders in the liturgical movement. Includes many wonderful photos.